# Harrog

## & Arou

**Malcolm Neesam**

When author Malcolm Neesam was asked where he wished to be born he chose Harrogate. It is a decision he has never regretted – and he has lived here ever since.

By profession Malcolm is a librarian. Following twenty years as County Music & Audiovisual Librarian for North Yorkshire, he cast loose as an independent researcher, writer and guide so as to make best use of his comprehensive knowledge of the town and its surrounding District. Now he is recognised as Harrogate's resident expert on all local matters – on its people, history, architecture, shopping and entertainments.

In addition to this Landmark City Guide to Harrogate Malcolm is a regular contributor to the Harrogate Advertiser and is also the author of several books on local history.

### – Preface –

This guidebook is very much a personal consideration of Harrogate and its attractions.

The author has received neither request nor payment for the inclusion of any of the amenities and businesses named or recommended in this guide. In particular, the author has a ferocious dislike of sullen shop assistants; impudent waiters; intrusive background music; religious hysterics; and people who use their cars as offensive weapons. Although the last two nuisances fall outside the remit of a guidebook, the first three do not, and users are encouraged to advise the author of any such encounters in establishments recommended within this book.

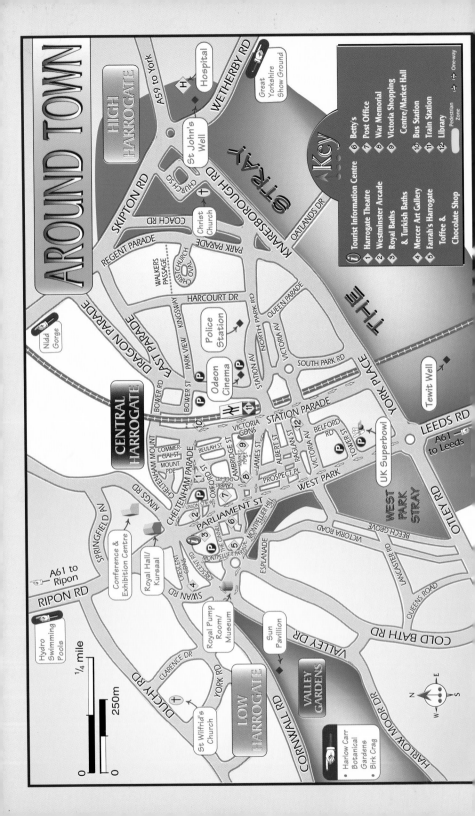

# CONTENTS

---

## Dedication

Dedicated by the author to the staff of the Harrogate Tourist Information Office.

# AUTHOR'S TOP TIPS

## ROYAL PUMP ROOM (see page 27)

### Crown Place
The 'symbol of Harrogate', dating from 1842. A beautiful building housing the strongest known sulphur well on Earth. The Harrogate Museum tells the story of the town's rise from a village to an internationally known spa.

## MERCER ART GALLERY (see page 28)

### Swan Road
Originally the Promenade Room, now converted into a splendid gallery to house a very fine art collection.

## BETTY'S CAFÉ (see page 39)

### Parliament Street
The ultimate 'tea shop' serving delicious meals and snacks in fine style. A range of teas, coffees, chocolates, cakes and bread are also on sale to take home. Forget your waistline, no visit to Harrogate is complete without a visit to Betty's.

## FARRAH'S HARROGATE TOFFEE SHOP (see page 38)

### Montpellier Parade
Unmissable retail emporium with dazzling displays of all kinds of delicious treats including the famous Harrogate Toffee made to a secret recipe.

## ROYAL BATHS (see page 19)

### Crescent Road
Once known as a 'cathedral of healing' this imposing building catered for the needs of both bathers and drinkers of the healing waters and was one of the largest hydrotherapy centres in the world.

## HARROGATE THEATRE (see page 45)

### Oxford Street
Restored late-Victorian interior with a superb art nouveau frieze by Francis Darlington in the entrance hall. Offers widely varied programme of theatrical entertainment.

## VALLEY GARDENS (see page 30)

Magnificent gardens which have grown up on the site of Bogs Field where 36 different mineral springs rise to the surface. Recreational facilities, wonderful floral displays, the Sun Colonnade, Magnesia Well café and occasional band concerts all contribute to visitors' enjoyment.

*Magnesia Well Café*

## THE KURSAAL (see page 23)

### Ripon Road
Now known as the Royal Hall, this turn of the century theatre has a beautiful interior much-beloved of film makers. Many famous names of the music world from classical to rock, big band to music hall, have appeared here.

## FOUNTAINS ABBEY (see page 68)

### (National Trust)
For an excursion near to Harrogate (10 miles) Fountains Abbey is superb. Here can be found the ruin of a 12th-century Cistercian abbey, an Elizabethan mansion and a glorious Georgian water garden. Beautiful walks in the surrounding deer park and an excellent visitor centre complete this World Heritage Site.

# Introduction

A line, drawn from John 0'Groats at the north-eastern tip of Scotland to Lands End at the south-western tip of England, finds Harrogate at its centre. Equally, a line from the western Irish Sea to the eastern North Sea also meets Harrogate half way. Harrogate is truly the heart of the island of Britain, as it is of England's biggest and finest county – Yorkshire. Indeed, what is England if not simply Yorkshire with fringes.

But Harrogate is more than the geographical centre of the nation, it is a District crammed with amenities to delight, enchant and entertain. Here are the beautiful and historic communities of Harrogate, Boroughbridge, Knaresborough, Masham, Pateley Bridge, and Ripon – to name only the largest. Here, glorious nature and the cunning artifice of man have combined to create landscapes which have been celebrated around the world by painters, such as Turner and Evans, and writers, including the Brontë sisters, and James Herriot.

Called England's golden triangle by the Financial Times , Harrogate is also a half hour's journey from vibrant Leeds, itself the fastest developing financial centre of the United Kingdom outside London, and York – peerless York – one of the world's best preserved and most historic ancient cities.

## Administrative area

Harrogate District was formed in 1974 when local government reorganisation combined the communities of Boroughbridge, Harrogate, Knaresborough, Masham, Pateley Bridge, and Ripon, along with several smaller villages, into a new authority based on Harrogate.

This District has a combined population of 150,000 people, of which about half live in Harrogate town. It comprises over 500 square miles, has 60,000 households, 7,000 businesses, 70 schools, 2 further and higher education colleges, and a large and flourishing voluntary sector.

From the cosmopolitan shopping streets of Harrogate, to the vast grandeur of its open moors, Harrogate District has variety and contrast at every turn. Much local employment lies within the sectors dedicated to serving visitors, and this – combined with a healthy retail climate, a little light manufacturing, and commuter activity with Leeds and York – ensures that the District is enhanced, rather than reduced, by local industry.

# Wells, parks and flowers

Harrogate is unique. No other known place on Earth possesses such a variety of Mineral Wells, there being some 89 officially recognised examples within the boundary of the town. In the so-called Bogs Field in Valley Gardens, 36 rise to the surface, some being separated only by a few feet of rock strata.

But Harrogate's uniqueness is not restricted to the Wells. The Stray, also known as the World's Biggest Lawn, surrounds the inner town, providing a green lung which can be admired as a thing of beauty, or as a practical means of encouraging bodily exercise. The Stray is also the setting for many of Harrogate's finest buildings, the grey-gold stone of which provides a pleasing contrast to the emerald green of over 200 acres of manicured grass.

St John's Well,
High Harrogate

But Harrogate is more than beauty, history and landscape. It is liveliness and sophistication, and if for some, the enjoyment of a lavish life-style appears too ostentatious, or the consumption of consumer goods too blatant a pursuit, then contrast is always available in the calm of the many parks and gardens of England's 'floral capital'.

Since 1963, the Harrogate International Festival has brought some of the world's greatest artists to Harrogate, usually during the summer months of July and August, when residents and visitors alike can experience one of England's finest artistic festivals.

Above all, Harrogate welcomes visitors, for its visitors have made Harrogate, and the whole place is dedicated to their wellbeing and pleasure.

# • HISTORY OF HARROGATE •

The earliest surviving spellings of Harrogate indicate an Anglo-Norse origin, the meaning of which was probably 'the road to Harlow' or 'the road to Haverah'. 'Harlow' Hill is Harrogate's highest point, the name of which may be found all over England, being Anglo-Norse for 'Soldiers' Hill'. 'Haverah' was the name of an ancient Royal Park, laid out in about 1100, which probably received its name from an even older geographical feature.

Whichever word provided the root for 'Harrogate', the 'gate' presents no problems, being Anglo-Norse for the 'way', or 'road'.

In its very earliest existence, 'Harrogate' was probably used as a name for a geographical feature or locality, as it does not appear in the Domesday Survey of 1086, although some of the communities which now form part of modern Harrogate are so listed: Bilton, Beckwith and Rossett.

The change of use of the name 'Harrogate' from a geographical name to that of a community, probably took place in the early 14th century, at a time when invaders from Scotland created much disruption in communities such as Boroughbridge, Knaresborough and Northallerton, causing a scattering of population.

By 1332, a Harrogate community is known to have existed.

## Royal Forest

Much of the modern Harrogate District once formed part of the great Royal Forest, which was created in about 1100 as a private estate for the King. With its northern boundary determined by the River Nidd, the Forest included Harrogate, Thruscross, Clint, Hampsthwaite and Killinghall.

In the forest's village communities, agricultural pursuits appear to have been pre-eminent, along with some iron-forging, and the occasional period of military duty in the King's service.

All this changed for Harrogate in 1571, when a Mr William Slingsby discovered a singular Iron Spring, bringing it to the attention of the medical profession. The great similarity of the mineral well with the famous one at Spa (in what is now Belgium) caused it to be dubbed the 'English Spa', or *Spadacrene Anglica*.

Trippers on the Stray

# England's first 'Spa'

Although the resort of Bath is older than Harrogate, being known to the Romans, Harrogate is nevertheless the first place in the British Isles to be given the name of 'Spa'. The Tudor government's obsession with Europe, seeing 'plottes and stratagems' behind every visit to Spa made by English visitors, led to the encouragement of visits to native resorts, and Harrogate – or the 'English Spa' – benefited in consequence.

There being no regular means of accommodating the earliest visitors to Harrogate, many lodged with the local farmers, who – being Yorkshiremen – soon discovered the profits which could be reaped from this new source. Gradually, the farmhouses were extended to accommodate the growing numbers of visitors, and indeed the origins of such great old Harrogate Hotels as the Dragon, Granby or Queen were those of the extended farmhouse.

The farms themselves provided visitors with choice provisions, as richness of table soon became a vital adjunct to the spa experience – despite the objections of the Doctors! The coming of the railways in the 1840s enabled fresh provisions to be imported and by the late-19th century, many of the farms attached to the hotels had been sold and developed into splendid housing estates, built in that solid and confident style so typical of the Victorian era.

**Above: There were fears that 'trippers' would lower the tone**
**Below: Spa rooms**

# Two Harrogates

Until 1860, there had been two Harrogates – High Harrogate, and Low Harrogate. High Harrogate, being elevated on a plateau, was where the first Iron Springs were discovered. Here were the three great Hotels, the Dragon, the Granby and the Queen. Here too, the first shops opened, many being London or York businesses who moved to Harrogate for the visitor 'season', which began when the roads improved in June, and ended when the weather began to deteriorate in late September.

## Hotel nicknames

High Harrogate's trio of great hotels had unusual nicknames. The Granby, because of its popularity with the aristocracy, was known as the 'House of Lords'; the Dragon, popular with the Military, gamblers, and 'fast' society, as the 'House of Commons'; and the Queen, frequented by wealthy merchants and traders, was dubbed 'The Manchester Warehouse'.

Harrogate's first custom built Theatre opened in High Harrogate in 1788, between the Library and the Granby Hotel, and accommodated the same actors who performed in the famous Georgian Theatre at Richmond – which, incidentally, opened in the same year.

Low Harrogate, situated in a valley at the point where roads to Bilton, Pannal, Leeds and Ripon met in proximity to the 'stinking wells', was always more irregular than High Harrogate, being inferior both in elevation and social status. Its single great hotel, the Crown, was nicknamed 'the hospital', because its proximity to the Sulphur Well made it popular with invalids.

# Rise of Low Harrogate

The changing fashion for Mineral Waters in the early-19th century, when the medical profession began to exploit the curative power of sulphur water, eventually saw the eclipse of High Harrogate by Low Harrogate. High Harrogate possessed only iron springs, whereas Low Harrogate possessed both iron and sulphur springs.

The change was marked in 1806, by the building of the town's first assembly room – today the Mercer Art Gallery – in Swan Road. Here, paying visitors could seek refuge in poor weather, read newspapers, listen to music, play cards, attend balls, indulge in flirtation – all perfectly acceptable pastimes at an English Spa.

Low Harrogate continued to develop throughout the 1820s and 1830s, with more Inns being established on West Park, Parliament Street and Cold Bath Road, many of which served trade from the important stage coach routes.

A suite of Baths, built in 1832 in what is now Crescent Gardens, further signified the importance of Low Harrogate.

Two years later, the owner of the Crown Hotel, Joseph Thackwray, built the Crown, or Montpellier Baths, in the gardens to the east of his Crown Hotel, on the site now occupied by the Royal Baths. The following year, 1835, saw a much bigger assembly room being opened at the corner of Ripon and King's Roads. Built in a noble Greek Doric style, the so-called 'Spa Rooms' became the centre of visitor entertainment at Harrogate for over a century.

## Local government

Until this time, Harrogate's government was in the hands of the so-called Vestry meetings, which consisted of members of the propertied classes meeting in

# Coming of the

The 1841 Harrogate Improvement Act enabled a new Royal Pump Room to be built, and various other enhancements to be effected. However, the next significant step in the town's growth was not produced by the Act, but by the coming of the railways.

The first of these connected Harrogate with the York & Midland Railway's line from Church Fenton and Wetherby, which opened in the summer of 1848, at the Brunswick Station on the Stray opposite Prince of Wales Mansions. The line from Leeds followed in 1849, with a terminus being opened at Starbeck.

The improved methods of transportation not only enabled more visitors to arrive in Harrogate, but also the

**Council Offices, Crescent Gardens, Low Harrogate**

# railways

importation of cheaper building materials, such as brick, and goods and supplies for the hotels and retailers. Before 1848, brick building was unknown in Harrogate, the town being built from stone supplied from the local quarries, which had been given along with the Stray and the Mineral Wells by King George III, in the great Award of 1778. After 1848, brick became more widely used, and within a short time, several local brickworks were established.

The changing times were not welcomed uniformly. There were fears that the railways would encourage the 'lower orders' to visit Harrogate, and that the noise of steam engines would depress the milk yield of local cattle!

the vestries of local churches. Their limited powers included responsibility for the local poor law, collection of the highways rates, and, occasionally, the enforcement of a levy for the militia.

All this changed after Joseph Thackwray's infamous attempt in 1835 to divert the Water of the Old Sulphur Well into the back of his Crown Hotel. The alarm this produced ensured sufficient public support for a new Act of Parliament, which not only provided Harrogate with new powers to protect the Mineral Wells, but also gave the town a new style of local government in the form of 21 elected Commissioners.

## Union of the two Harrogates

An important initiative was launched in 1860 by a group of local businessmen, with the establishment of the Victoria Park Company. The company planned the construction of a new town centre, which would link up the two ancient villages of High and Low Harrogate by means of a series of residential and retailing streets. The heart of the scheme consisted of Victoria Avenue, which ran from High Harrogate's Queen Parade, down to West Park, overlooking Low Harrogate.

At right angles to this, the railway line was brought into central Harrogate, with a new central station being opened in 1862. Harrogate's population had grown from about 1,500 in 1801, to about 5,500 by the time the new Central Railway Station opened. The next few decades witnessed an unparalleled rate of growth, with the town's population rising to about 10,000 by the time of Incorporation as a Borough in 1884.

An important new suite of Baths, the New Victoria Baths, was built by the Improvement Commissioners in Crescent Gardens. Opened in 1871, the building still stands, in modified form, being the Council Offices or surrogate Town Hall.

Queen Victoria's grant of a Borough Charter in 1884 further stimulated Harrogate's growth. The new Council, with its Mayor and Aldermen, included some of the most brilliant, far-sighted, and

## England's Klondike

In 1874, a new Market Hall was built, directly opposite the Central Railway Station, which enabled the growing residential population to buy those foodstuffs which hitherto had been snapped up by the hotels. So much development occurred in Harrogate between this time and the First World War, that the town was nicknamed the Klondike of England.

energetic men ever to place themselves at the service of the community, the Carter brothers, George Dawson, Richard Ellis, Charles Fortune, Samson Fox, to name only the most dynamic.

## Climax of an era

A great period of development opened in 1897, year of Queen Victoria's Diamond Jubilee, and the zenith of British Imperial power and prestige. The Royal Baths, a virtual cathedral to health, was opened on 3 July 1897, as Europe's most advanced centre for hydrotherapeutic treatment.

It was followed two years later, by the splendid Opera House, which today houses Harrogate's lively Theatre. Also in 1900, the great Hotel Majestic, crowned with a mighty copper dome, first opened its doors for the reception of guests.

In 1903, a second monster hotel, the Grand, went up overlooking Valley Gardens, and on 28 May 1903, the Kursaal – or Cure-Hall – was opened by Sir Hubert Parry, as the town's principal place of entertainment. All this investment was to support the Spa Ritual, which had developed over the centuries.

## Changing times

Following the catastrophe of the 1914-18 war, Harrogate's clientele changed. Greater numbers of visitors poured into town, but they had less individual wealth than the select few who had patronised the pre-war Spa. The Council set about making Harrogate more attractive to a wider range of visitors, and although grave doubts were expressed about the wisdom of attracting the 'charabanc trade', the town's attractions were broadened and enhanced!

The 1930s saw the opening of the popular Sun Colonnade and Pavilion in Valley Gardens, the construction of a new market hall, bus station and a significant enlargement of treatment facilities at the Royal Baths. World War Two ensured that this last improvement could not be put to the test.

The war years saw many government departments being moved up to Harrogate, such as the Air Ministry and Post Office, and at the war's end, it was obvious that Harrogate faced profound change. The advent of the National Health Service, the wholesale distribution of wealth throughout British society –

**Alfresco music at the Harrogate Festival**

combined with the growing habit of foreign holidays, and a general belief that Spas were out-of-date, all meant that in Britain, the Spa began to decline.

## Conferences and exhibitions

In Harrogate, the Council moved quickly and by the mid-1950s, the town had begun to transform itself into a modern exhibition and conference centre. The Rose Gardens, which formerly ran along King's Road, were sacrificed, and a series of economically successful Exhibition Halls were built, a process which culminated in the controversial Conference Centre which opened in 1981.

The Commercial success of these ventures encouraged further developments, both by the Council as well as the private sector. The Council restored many of the old Spa buildings, filling them with new life, and the private sector continues to invest in Harrogate.

Today, the visitor has only to walk through the streets of central Harrogate to see evidence for this continuing faith in the future of a town whose modern motto – *To be of service* – is testimony to the continuing importance accorded to the visitor. And let all visitors know this – *you are important – your welfare is important, to the whole of the Harrogate District.*

**A startling sight at the summer Festival**

# The Great Yorkshire Show

**O**ne of the most exciting and popular events held in Harrogate is the annual Great Yorkshire Show – a cornucopia of country life with exciting ring displays, more than 8,000 different animals (everything from bulls to bunnies!) – and a vast array of stands selling every conceivable item.

Held on the 350 acre permanent site on the Wetherby Road (A661) just 2 miles from the centre of town, the show is held each year in early/mid July and attracts over 100,000 visitors from across Britain.

Line upon line of pedigree cattle, sheep and pigs, more than 1,000 horses and ponies, coupled with fashion shows, demonstrations of country skills such as stick carving and dry stone walling, ensure that there is something to interest everyone.

The Main Ring is the heart of the event. Here marching military bands, the Musical Display by The Household Cavalry, the elegance of horse drawn coaches and the thrills and spills of international show jumping and much much more, never fail to delight. The Flower Show is always a magnet whether you're a gardener or not, and then there's all the fun of the Theakston Summer Fest.

Elsewhere the latest farming technology can be seen, courtesy of the north's leading universities, whilst the delights of country life can be experienced in the Country Pursuits Area. Have a go at fly fishing, try your hand at gun dog training, or simply marvel at the awe inspiring birds of prey. Check out the James Mackay's Ferret Show – he maintains they really are loveable creatures who have simply had a bad press, but see for yourself!

But if all the action gets too much, the woodland walk provides the ideal place for a break.

A free shuttle bus between Harrogate Railway Station and the Showground operates on each day of the Show, with buses leaving in each direction approximately every twenty minutes.

Parking is free and extensive. Tickets on the gate cost approximately £11 for adults; £8.50 for over 60s and £5.50 for children. There are discounts for tickets booked in advance, for example a family ticket (two adults and two children) costs £25.

Whatever your interest, the Great Yorkshire Show is an excellent day out – but be warned, a one day visit may not be enough! For further details on the Show please ring 01423 541000.

A detailed look at the town of Harrogate is most easily accomplished by dividing it into three areas: Low Harrogate which includes the Spa area and Valley Gardens; Central Harrogate; and High Harrogate.

THE ROYAL BATHS

# • LOW HARROGATE SPA AREA •

Crescent Gardens is a good place to begin a tour of Harrogate, as it is surrounded with monuments to the historic Spa, and contains an attractive expanse of grass and flower bedding. One of the differences between England and France is that in France, grass is to be looked at whereas, in England, it is to be walked on – and this is certainly true in Harrogate.

Stand on the grass of Crescent Gardens and look north towards the former New Victoria Baths, built in 1871, and converted in 1930 into the Council's **Municipal Buildings**. Above the handsome classical frontage may be seen the old motto of Harrogate '*Arx celebris fontibus*' – a citadel famous for its springs.

## Royal Baths

Nearly opposite, to the south, stands the imposing edifice of the **Royal Baths**, opened in 1897 by Queen Victoria's grandson, HRH The Duke of Cambridge. Above the lead dome flies a golden cockerel, symbol of health since the time of the ancient Greeks. Within, it is still possible to sample the famous Turkish Baths, whose setting resembles an oriental palace, or a scene from Alice in Wonderland.

At the time of writing, the whole elaborate complex is subject to a planning application, which demonstrates the faith of the private sector in the future of Harrogate. The plan is to construct a new spa centre, along with high-quality restaurants and wine bars, plus a new office for Harrogate's Tourist Information department.

On entering the former Grand Pump Room of the Royal Baths, the visitor will understand why this building was once known as a cathedral of healing, or temple to Hygeia! Lofty columns support a great coffered dome, beneath which, on the cornice, may be seen a finely lettered inscription, taken from James Thompson's poem *Castle of Indolence*:

*Ah! What avail the largest gifts of Heaven*

*When drooping health and spirits go amiss,*

*How tastless then whatever can be given,*

*Health is the vital principal of bliss, and*

*Exercise of Health*

# Harrogate Waters and the Spa Experience

## THE HARROGATE WATERS

We are told that, when the average bottle of water is opened, it's contents have been through the human body at least seven times before coming into our hands. Rainfall is collected, used, then passing into the sewerage system from our homes, schools and factories, it is eventually purified, and finally returned to the sea and land before evaporating and becoming cloud once more. Thus the cycle goes on, endlessly.

But Harrogate water is not the result of rain, or precipitation. It is rather the result of magmatic activity, deep beneath the crust of the Earth. Granite, as it sinks into molten magma, gives off molecules of water vapour, which rise as superheated steam, before condensing into water. When this vapour condenses in layers of minerals, it appropriates the mineral, and becomes a true mineral water.

Geological activity can result in layers of different mineral strata being tilted into a vertical position, and when this occurs, the mineral waters flow to the surface as springs. Harrogate waters include many ancient and deep-seated springs, and as such, they are a miracle of nature.

Indeed, more unique natural mineral springs rise to the surface of the Earth in Harrogate than at any other known place on the planet. As such, Harrogate is globally unique, and should be classified as a World Heritage Site.

## STOP PRESS – WATER BOTTLING PLANT AND VISITOR CENTRE

At the time of going to press, plans have been published to construct a modern plant for the bottling of Harrogate's celebrated pure table waters. To be built on Harlow Moor Road, at the northern boundary of the Pinewoods, the new centre looks set to be a valuable addition to the town's attractions, as well as being a vital part of the programme of Spa revival.

## THE SPA RITUAL OF FORMER TIMES

Newly arrived at an inn or hotel, the visitor would be attended by the establishment's doctor, who – after an interview and examination – would prescribe a specific course of mineral water.

On his first full morning, the visitor would be awakened at 6.00am, then take a full hour to be dressed, by a servant, to the exacting requirements of high fashion. Properly attired, but

Drinking the Waters

After drinking the Waters

without having breakfasted, the visitor would then walk down to the Royal Pump Room, the environs of which were completely free of all vehicular traffic.

Entering the Royal Pump Room, the visitor would pass over the doctor's prescription, being handed in return a prescribed dosage of mineral water, to be consumed on the spot. This was often performed with extreme reluctance! A walk was then necessary, usually through neighbouring Crescent Gardens, where a band performed for the delight of the visitors, and where society could be ogled, and fashions admired.

## ROYAL VISITORS

In just one of those pre-First World War seasons, the company included Queen Alexandra, King Manuel and Queen Amelia of Portugal, Prince Henry of Prussia (the Kaiser's brother), Prince Christopher of Greece, about half of the British Imperial cabinet, and the usual smattering of Maharajas and Archdukes.

## AMUSEMENTS BY DAY...

After a little exercise, the visitor returned to his hotel, consumed breakfast, and obeyed the single most important instruction from the Doctor – *stay in,* for at least two hours. This was necessary, as some of the Harrogate waters were – and are – a strong purge!

Late morning would see visits to the shops, followed after luncheon, by an outing to some beauty spot such as Fountains Abbey, Knaresborough or Ripley, travelling either by coach and horses, or – after 1900 – by motor car.

## ... AND BY NIGHT!

Dinner in the evening was often a lavish affair, with as many as 14 different courses being served, and this could be followed by a visit to the Kursaal, possibly to hear Melba sing, Kreisler play or Elgar conduct. Not that there was ever only a single choice, as Harrogate provided a wide range of attractions for the delight of its visitors.

And for those visitors in need of more advanced Spa amenities, the Royal Baths provided the greatest variety of specialised hydrotherapeutic treatments of any Spa in the world.

## St George Hotel

Opposite the main entrance to the Royal Baths, the grand old **St George Hotel** rises up proudly, at the junction with the busy Ripon Road. The St George was originally a humble cottage property, which after 1778 began to develop as an Inn convenient both for travellers and the Sulphur Wells, and which eventually expanded to fill the entire corner site.

On 9 May 1910, from the hotel's ground floor bay window overlooking Crescent Gardens, the Grand Duchess George of Russia and Princess Victoria, sister to the King, watched the proclamation of George V as King and Emperor, being read from the steps of the Royal Baths before an immense and ecstatic crowd.

The singular mound at the Ripon Road boundary of Crescent Gardens contains an elaborate floral clock, presented to the town on 9 January 1999 by the Harrogate International Toy and Christmas Fair and the Harrogate International Centre.

## Cupid & Psyche

Within the little glass pavilion, used to display Harrogate's contribution to the Gateshead Garden Festival of 1990, is the lovely statue of Cupid and Psyche; carved by Italian sculptor Giavanni Benzoni, originally set up in the Spa Rooms Gardens in c1870.

When the gardens of the former Spa Rooms were removed in 1958, for the building of the first exhibition hall, the statue was put into storage, and subsequently lost. A chance discovery in a council depot, 30 years later, brought Cupid and Psyche to light.

# Kursaal

Across the Ripon Road, Harrogate's principal exhibition, conference and entertainment facilities may be found, of which the architecturally flamboyant **Kursaal, or Royal Hall**, is the most immediately obvious. The gorgeous marble and plaster interior designed by Frank Matcham, England's greatest designer of theatres, has proved irresistible to film makers, such as Ken Russell who shot here much of his infamous film about Richard Strauss.

Some of the famous names to have appeared on the Kursaal's stage include: –

**Comedians**
Dan Leno, Vesta Tilley, George Robey, Little Tich, Harry Lauder and Laurel and Hardy;

**Composers**
Bantock, Busoni, Dohnanyi, Elgar, German, Parry, Ethyl Smyth, Stanford, Vaughan Williams;

**Singers**
Clara Butt, Walter Widdop, John McCormack, Nellie Melba, Paul Robeson, Gracie Fields, Richard Tauber;

**Band leaders**
Billy Cotton, Jack Payne, Carol Gibbons, Joe Loss, Jack Hylton, Roy Fox, Henry Hall; the dancer Pavlova;

**and** the clown Grock, the explorer Shackleton, the actress Sarah Bernhardt, the Beatles, and the Rolling Stones, who made their first Harrogate appearance in April 1920!

# Opulent hotels

Many views of Low Harrogate are dominated by the awesome **Hotel Majestic**, which looms over the Ripon Road, north of the Kursaal. Opened in 1900, the Majestic was the last word in Victorian opulence. With its striking red brick facade, and high copper dome, the Hotel Majestic forms as splendid a backdrop to Low Harrogate as the former Grand Hotel does to Valley Gardens.

The Majestic has the dubious honour of being the only building in Harrogate to have been bombed in the Second World War, by a single Nazi raider. There is no proof to support the local story that the pilot dropped his bomb (which failed to go off) in revenge for having been refused admittance to the hotel before the war, on account of his dinner jacket not being up to Harrogate standards!

Opposite the Hotel Majestic, on the western side and crown of Ripon Road, rises the large **Cairn Hotel**, built in 1889 as the Cairn Hydro Hotel, Harrogate's second speciality Hydro Hotel – the Old Swan was the first. After recent refurbishment, the Cairn is again a popular location with visitors.

**Hotel Majestic**

## The Academy

Even the top London health clubs find it hard to rival the superb facilities of the discreetly named **Academy**, which is quite simply a magnificent and exclusive private health club. Housed in an interesting building which formerly contained the Municipal Electricity Works, and located on the northern fringes of the town, at Oakdale Place, The Academy's swimming pool, tennis courts, gymnasium,

## Harrogate Hydro

Opened in the spring of 1999 as Harrogate's state of the art swimming pool, the Harrogate Hydro in Jennyfield Drive has a 25 metre, eight-lane pool, a separate teaching pool, an activity pool with diving facilities and moveable floor. Separate facilities for spectators are provided, as well as catering, and additional features include a crèche, a studio for dancing and aerobics, a fitness suite, and a meeting room. Access is available either by means of a pass, or a 'pay & play' ticket. Admission is generally from 7.30am to 9.30pm, although it is sensible to check times in advance of arrival. For further information, ☎ 01423 556767.

## Moving on

Returning down Ripon Road to Crescent Gardens, the visitor will pass a new Italian restaurant, **Joe Rigatoni's**, opened in November 1998, after a lengthy and lavish programme of reconstruction, and which promises to be a welcome addition to the town's range of speciality restaurants.

health and beauty suites, aerobics, crèche and nursery provide health-seekers with their ultimate requirements.

At the time of writing, three Harrogate hotels – the Balmoral, the Rudding Park, and Grants Hotel – can arrange for their guests to visit The Academy. Other hotels, such as the St George and Majestic, provide 'Spa' amenities of their own.

South of the Majestic, and next to the Kursaal, once stood the **Spa Rooms** built in 1835 in the form of a noble Doric Temple, which for over a century was Low Harrogate's principal assembly room. Dismantled in 1939, the site is earmarked for a new exhibition hall, the appearance of which has been a cause célèbre in the town.

Further east along Kings Road may be found the exhibition halls and the great **Harrogate International Centre**, flanked by the mirrored glass tower block of the **Moat House Hotel.** Both buildings were the result of a controversial development in the 1970s which was designed to ensure Harrogate's pre-eminence as a Conference and Exhibition centre. When it finally opened in 1981, the Harrogate International Centre had cost an estimated £34 million.

Returning along King's Road to the east. After passing the recently re-opened and much-praised **Oliver's 24** Restaurant – whose Scandinavian repertoire includes the author's favourite pickled Herrings, as well as a much wider menu – and the popular Wine Bar, **Christie's**, at the junction with Cheltenham Parade, Crescent Gardens may again be reached.

## Charles Dickens on Harrogate

It was within the Spa Rooms, on 11 September 1858, that Charles Dickens gave his famous reading. In describing the event to his daughter, he said that Harrogate was *"the queerest place, with the strangest people in it, leading the oddest lives of dancing, newspaper reading and tables d'hôte"*.

## Nightlife

Housed in the former Spa Hotel – an uncouth building of 1900 – at the junction of Kings Road and Cheltenham Crescent, **Jimmy's Nightclub** is highly popular with a clientele which enjoys loud music, crowded rooms, flashing lights, and ample liquid refreshment.

The author must admit that he has only viewed the premises at 10.00am one Monday morning, and that his experience of the club's opening hours is the result of passing Jimmy's in a taxi, with its windows up, during a rain storm. However, as the often lengthy queues attest, Jimmy's has a large, enthusiastic and largely youthful clientele, to whom it may with confidence be commended.

## Exhibition and conference facilities

Harrogate has been a venue for conferences and exhibitions since the 1870s, but it is only since the Second World War that the town has made a deliberate attempt to develop this business as its principal industry. The Kings Road **exhibition halls**, built after 1958, are the most obvious outward manifestation of this trend.

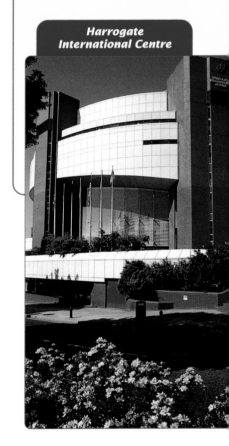

**Harrogate International Centre**

The exhibition halls provide a total of 15,000sq m (gross) display space, and the business as a whole produced an income of £108 million during the 1997-8 financial year. Regular visitors include the Toy Fair, the Home and Gift Exhibition, the National Floor Show (Carpets and Floor Coverings), the Bridal Wear Fair, and the Theatre Nurses Exhibition.

The **Harrogate Centre**, with its impressive interior ramp reminiscent of New York's Guggenheim Gallery, has been host to such events as the Eurovision Song Contest, the Institute of Personnel and Development Conference, and the Chartered Institute of Housing. With its 2,000-seater auditorium, the Centre possesses state of the art facilities including those for broadcasting, translation and security. The building is also used for the Harrogate International Festival, and can accommodate the largest of orchestras and choirs.

## Old Swan Hotel & beyond

**Crescent Gardens** lead north, via Swan Road, to the **Old Swan Hotel**, set in beautiful gardens overlooking the Royal Pump Room. The missing novelist Agatha Christie was discovered at this celebrated old establishment, in December 1926, after her disappearance had produced one of the biggest 'manhunts' of the century. The film *Agatha*, starring Vanessa Redgrave and Dustin Hoffman, was partly filmed here.

The Old Swan's origins are 18th century, although the principal impression gained by today's visitor is of 19th century opulence. Swan Road is lined with attractive Georgian and Victorian terraces, several of which include hotels, of which **Grants Hotel**, with its fine Chimney Pots Restaurant, and the long established **Studley Hotel**, are outstandingly good.

Three interesting businesses lie between the Mercer Art Gallery and Hales Bar, at the junction with Crescent Road. The first is the private **Anstey Gallery**, whose displays often feature fascinating works of sculpture. Next may be found **Country Corner**, an attractive shop specialising in high quality country clothing.

Finally, the **Old Coffee Shop**, a rare survivor of the traditional English café, where the customer may enjoy excellent catering, in one of the best locations of any café in Harrogate, looking out upon the Royal Pump Room and Valley Gardens.

## Royal Pump Room

The beautiful copper-domed **Royal Pump Room**, which stands at the heart of Low Harrogate, where Crescent Road, Swan Road, Well Hill and Valley Gardens all meet, was built by the Harrogate Improvement Commissioners in 1842. Designed with an octagonal ground plan, by Harrogate born Isaac Thomas Shutt, the Royal Pump Room is the symbol of Harrogate.

# Mercer Art Gallery

Half way between the Old Swan and the Royal Pump Room, the **Mercer Art Gallery** may be seen, occupying a building of 1806. This was once the Promenade Room, built as a place of assembly for visitors resorting to the Spa. An elaborate conversion, finished in 1991, provides splendid accommodation for Harrogate's wonderful art collections, which include works by Atkinson Grimshaw, Frith, Turner, and Bernard Evans. **Not to be missed on any account**. Admission free.

Today, the Royal Pump Room contains the **Harrogate Museum**, but the building's original purpose was to house drinkers at the famous 'Old Sulphur Well' – the strongest known sulphur well on Earth. This may still be seen through a glass window in the floor, which reveals the original well head and its sulphur water. Visitors should note that what appears to be a concrete surface is in fact the surface of the sulphur water, which, occasionally, gives notice of its presence by bubbling.

The main entrance to the Royal Pump Room Museum is on the Crown Parade section of the annexe, built in 1913 as extra accommodation for the water drinkers. This annexe is itself worthy of note, as it was built of special light-weight materials, in order to avoid harming the geological strata through which the sulphur waters rise. The annexe was opened, amid scenes of great pomp and circumstance, by the Lord Mayor of London.

## Old Betty

Around the Sulphur Well may be seen several figures, one of which – complete with water ladle – is Betty Lupton, the Queen of the well. Elizabeth Lupton, better known as 'Old Betty', dispensed the Harrogate Waters to visitors for over 60 years, when she was a great celebrity, renowned both for her loyalty of service, and for the garrulity of her conversation! She died on 22 August 1843, having lived long enough to see the Old Sulphur Well subjected to several rebuildings.

## Harrogate Museum

Visitors should take time to examine the finely carved octagonal counter, which now functions as the Museum's entrance desk, from which tickets of admission may be obtained. Beyond, the museum contains an attractive representation of aspects of street life in old Harrogate, with transport, children's games and shop windows, as well as displays featuring spa life.

Walking round to the left, the visitor will arrive in the old 1842 building, which contains – among other exhibits – the sulphur well. As with most museums, Harrogate's has more artefacts than it can exhibit at one time, so displays change frequently. The little shop sells a good range of Harrogate souvenirs.

Beneath the great dome of the 1842 room, an attractive window of rare etched glass may be seen. This window was erected in 1870 as a memorial to members of the Slingsby family, of Scriven. Designed and executed by Pilkington's of St Helens, the window depicts the troubling of the waters of the Pool of Siloam.

# • VALLEY GARDENS AREA •

Valley Gardens, so-called because it is simply gardens in a Valley, has at its heart the historic 'Bogs Field'. Here many Mineral Wells rise to the surface, formerly producing marshy or boggy conditions. In the 18th century, a footpath between the Old Sulphur Well and the Bogs Field became popular with visitors; this was embellished by the Victorians in the middle of the 19th century, who planted trees and shrubs to enhance the walk. From this humble beginning has grown the present magnificence of the Valley Gardens.

The original footpath, which runs from the main entrance on Well Hill, is known as the 'Elgar Walk', in honour of the many visits made to Harrogate before 1927 by Sir Edward Elgar, Great Britain's greatest composer. The adjoining stream is home to greedy ducks, whom children delight in feeding!

At the end of the Elgar walk, the **Magnesia Well Café** may be seen, a pretty, copper roofed, circular building of 1895, which in summer is swathed with hanging flower baskets. Behind the Magnesia Well Café may be found the little **Boating Lake**, popular with sailors of all ages.

*The former 'Bogs Field' circle, now the heart of Valley Gardens*

The circular flower beds opposite – the heart of Bogs Field – contain the greatest known selection of unique Mineral Waters on the face of the Earth. Thirty-six different springs rise to the surface, once being piped down to the Royal Baths for use in the various treatments. Most of the well-heads were sunk beneath the grass in about 1971, when the Spa was moribund, but two of the circular 'caps' still remain.

## Sun Pavilion

To the north, Valley Gardens is bounded by the long and classical **Sun Colonnade**, which leads to the delightful **Sun Pavilion**, opened in 1933 as an attraction both for visitors and invalids.

After being thoroughly refurbished in the late 1990s, the Sun Pavilion was re-opened by Her Majesty, Queen Elizabeth II, on 10 December 1998. Today's visitors can still relish something of the original art deco atmosphere. Do not be surprised to see Fred Astaire and Ginger Rogers come dancing down the stairs from Cornwall Road!

Although the Sun Pavilion is now used largely for private functions, it is occasionally open to the general public, especially in summer. The great stained glass dome is worthy of notice.

Cornwall Road, which forms the northern boundary to Valley Gardens, includes the enormous stone building of the former Grand Hotel, now **Windsor House**, which opened as an hotel in 1903. Following its occupation in the Second World War by Government Departments, the Grand failed to re-establish itself as an hotel, and now contains several prestigious office suites.

Beyond the Sun Pavilion to the south-west, the **Bog Garden** contains a collection of marsh plants, and the little gothic pump room of 1858 which served the waters of the **Old Magnesia Well**.

## Charitable healing

The great national charitable institution of the **Royal Bath Hospital** once overlooked this part of Valley Gardens. Opened in 1824, the Royal Bath Hospital provided the sick-poor of the United Kingdom with a charitable medical service. The hospital removed to Leeds in 1994, the old buildings being subsequently adapted for residential use by Crosby Homes, a development known as **Sovereign Court**.

Much of the gardens between the site of the former Royal Bath Hospital, and Valley Drive, are dedicated to games and sports such as tennis and miniature golf, and also to the childrens' play area, with its paddling pool, swings and dog-free zone.

# Harlow Carr Botanical Gardens

The footpath which leads south-west of Bogs Field, leads to the pretty **Pine Woods**, which in turn (about one and a quarter miles) lead to the world-famous **Harlow Carr Botanical Gardens**. Run by the Northern Horticultural Society, Harlow Carr Botanical Gardens were developed on this exposed open moorland after the Second World War.

To reach the gardens on foot, the hard-surfaced path should be followed from Bogs Field up Harlow Hill, until it terminates at the **Ex-Service Men's Memorial**, a simple stone crucifix set amidst shrubs and trees, erected after the First World War by ex-service men and their dependants.

At this point, the footpath divides in three routes, and the walker should take the middle path – unsurfaced – and follow it through the Pine Woods until Harlow Moor Drive is reached. Crossing this road, the footpath leads through a short section of the Pine Woods, before reaching the grassy clearing, popular in summer for picnic parties. The footpath skirts the clearing's lower edge, until it joins the asphalt path which leads down to Crag Lane and the entrance to Harlow Carr Botanical Gardens.

The extensive areas of beds are interspersed with magnificent trees, shrubs and woodlands, at the heart of which is a stream, or beck. One attraction is no less than the **National Collection of Rhubarb!** Here, too, is a fine research library, museum of gardening, model village and restaurant. Visitors may also purchase from the gift shop and plant centre.

The gardens, to which an admission fee is charged, are not typical formal gardens, with beds of geraniums and petunias. They are 68 acres of trial, or experimental gardens, the philosophy being that if a plant will grow here, it will grow anywhere in the north of England!

Beyond the stream, in the woods, the visitor will come across a clearing in which stand six magnificent Doric columns. These come from the historic Spa Rooms, dismantled in 1939, which stood in Low Harrogate next to the Royal Hall, or Kursaal.

Visitors in the summer should look out for the occasional plays which are enacted on the greensward at Harlow Carr – travelling actors perform Shakespeare before an audience of picnickers of both human and insect variety.

# St Wilfrid's Church

**A**dmirers of fine English Churches must not fail to visit St Wilfrid's, located in Duchy Road, about eight minutes walk from Valley Gardens. Walk up Cornwall Road from Well Hill, and turn right into Clarence Drive, heading away from Valley Gardens. Continue along Clarence Drive, across York Road, and past the substantial buildings of Harrogate Ladies College, until Clarence Drive meets Duchy Road. Turn left, and St Wilfrid's Church is then the second building on the left.

### SIR JOHN BETJEMAN ON ST WILFRID'S

The bald facts are that this church was built for the new 'Duchy Estate', between 1908 and 1935, to a design by Temple Moore, in the early English style of architecture. Facts, however, can not convey the sublime proportions and noble harmony of this superb edifice, which can only be experienced by personal examination. The windows, by Victor Milner, harmonise with the structure of the great church, with particular skill. If Harrogate ever has need of a Cathedral, this is it. Beloved by Sir John Betjeman, who wrote:

> O, I wad gang tae Harrogate
> Tae a kirk by Temple Moore,
> Wi a tall choir and a lang nave
> And rush mats on the floor;
> And Percy Dearmer chasubles
> And nae pews but chairs,
> And there we'll sing the Sarum rite
> *Tae English Hymnal airs*

# Birk Crag

Harlow Carr Gardens have their main entrance in Crag Lane, which forms the south-western boundary of the Pine Woods. Passing the entrance, and walking along Crag Lane in a north-westerly direction, the visitor will soon arrive at **Birk Crag.**

Historian William Grainge, in 1871, called this *"the grandest piece of scenery in the neighbourhood. On a fine day when the heath is in bloom with the sunshine streaming over it, thick woods rising darkly on the west, the brook stealing into view from under an arcade of foliage, and winding along the bottom in graceful curves, it forms a picture at once wild, grand and beautiful"*. The exposed rock formations provide a delightful picnic spot.

Visitors on foot, wishing to vary their return route to the Valley Gardens entrance, may, in Crag Lane, continue due south until the junction with the busy Otley Road is reached. At this point the footpath turns sharp left, leading up to the crown of Harlow Hill. The handsome stone house on the right, Beckwith Knowle, is now home to a superior establishment, the **Pine Marten**, where refreshments may be obtained.

# Harlow Hill & Well Hill

Beyond this, the crown of Harlow Hill is filled with All Saints Church and its imposing cemetery, houses and playing fields. Turning sharp left at the eastern boundary of the playing field, is the **Panoramic Walk**, which on a clear day provides the visitor with splendid views towards the Hambledon Hills and York.

This footpath passes between the water tower, at right, and at left, the tall square shaft of the Observation Tower of c1829, which is no longer open to the public. The path then continues through the nurseries, before again joining the Pine Woods

Valley Gardens main entrance lies on **Well Hill**, overlooking the Royal Pump Room, where several Georgian lodging houses still stand, now in private occupation.

## Open-air sculpture

In recent years the entrance to Valley Gardens has been dominated by free standing sculptures, erected by Harrogate's Mercer Art Gallery, on short term loan from their owners. During their few months of display, these sculptures invariably attract much comment, especially in the columns of the local newspaper!

# • LOW HARROGATE SHOPPING AREA •

## Nearby shops, restaurants & hotels

Walking from Well Hill and passing the Royal Pump Room, the visitor will see, at right, **Royal Parade**, a curving terrace of exclusive shops and restaurants, built after 1847. At left, the pleasant tree-lined **Crown Place**, scene of Joseph Thackwray's infamous 1835 'Well Case', and today, the lively **Court's Bar**, which often boasts a resident pianist.

At the end of Crown Place, across Crescent Road, **Hales Bar** comes into view. The bar to the right of the main entrance contains original early-19th century fitments, complete with gas lighting.

**Royal Parade**, a development of the 1840s, received its name from the habit of distinguished visitors promenading round the environs of the Old Sulphur Well. Today, Royal Parade is home to several handsome antiques businesses, as well as the delightful **Old Bell Tavern** which re-opened in 1999 after a gap of 184 years, following closure of the original Bell Inn on this exact site, in 1815. The dining room is on the first floor, above the ground floor ale and wine bar.

Royal Parade has always been known for its antique shops, which contribute greatly to the area's attractive window displays. Also on Royal Parade is the well-established and popular **Café Fleur**, which operates in a completely smoke-free environment, for which it was given the Roy Castle Gold Award.

**The gas-lit Hales Bar – a popular traditional pub**

## Crown Hotel

Opposite Royal Parade rises the great building of the **Crown Hotel**, which for centuries was Low Harrogate's most important address. Known in the 19th century by its nickname, 'the Hospital', because of its popularity with genuine invalids, the Crown was always convenient for the Old Sulphur Well.

Lord Byron stayed here in 1806, arriving with a 'string of horses, dogs and mistresses'. Did Branwell Brontë really plan to elope from the Crown with his beloved Lydia Robinson? We will probably never know for certain. More recently, the Crown featured in the delightful reminiscences of Alan Bennett.

Most of the principal frontage of the Crown Hotel dates from 1847, with the wings being added after 1870.

---

The pretty, flower-covered roundabout outside the Crown Hotel forms the junction of **Cold Bath Road**, at right, and **Montpellier Parade**, at left. The former takes its name from the Cold Well which was once in regular demand, and is lined with an interesting mixture of former inns, shops and residential properties.

The most splendid of these is the **White Hart Hotel**, a magnificent neo-classical structure of 1847, justly popular with discerning visitors, as a lovely and conveniently central hotel. A couple of blocks beyond the White Hart and further up Cold Bath Road, lies **William & Victoria's** wine bar and restaurant – a popular and busy meeting place.

**Montpellier Parade**, to the left of Crown roundabout, begins at the tiny octagonal **White Cottage**, now a shop, once built as ticket office for the gardens of the Crown Hotel. Before investigating the delights of Montpellier Parade, the visitor should examine **Montpellier Gardens** and **Montpellier Mews**.

## Harrogate's antique quarter

Opposite the White Cottage, at the corner with Montpellier Parade, **Tennant's**, the auctioneers, have their Harrogate headquarters, next to which stands the **Walker Gallery** (also round the corner at 13a Montpellier Parade) with their displays of fine paintings.

The famous **Drum and Monkey** – a fish restaurant, so heavily patronised, that bookings are often required – adjoins further interesting businesses, of which the long established antiques firms of **Charles Lumb & Sons**, and the neighbouring **Thorntons of Harrogate**, are distinguished examples.

Devotees of female high fashion should not fail to investigate **Morgan Clare**, run by Su and Martin Allard, which displays the best of British design for women. Given the prestigious *Best New Store* award for 1997-8, and nominated for the *Top Fifty to watch* 1998-9, by *Real Business* Magazine, this young company has become another Harrogate success story.

---

## The Rink

Enthusiasts of antique furniture should not leave Harrogate without first visiting a fine old Harrogate institution, **Smiths' – the Rink – Ltd**, specialists in both 'period and modern' furniture.

Housed in a former skating rink in Dragon Road, near to the large ASDA store, Smiths has, throughout its long existence, sold much of the old and massive furniture of Victorian and Edwardian Harrogate, as well as other periods. To walk through its display rooms is to savour something of the tastes and fashions of other times, as well as those of our own age.

---

Montpellier Gardens runs into Montpellier Mews, which contains several attractive and high quality establishments. **And So To Bed** provides a fascinating selection of bedroom furniture and fittings, often of unusual design. The adjoining **Lords Restaurant**, decorated with cricketing memorabilia, is widely regarded as being amongst the best half-dozen in town.

Opposite is the **Montpellier Mews,** an attractive development of former stables and bath chair garaging. The **Antique Market** comprises several private antiques businesses housed under one roof, where the visitor is free to walk without compunction to buy. The adjoining **Millers – the Bistro** is another Harrogate restaurant – a fish specialist – which is recommended with confidence. Retracing the path to Montpellier Parade, via Montpellier Gardens, the visitor is now ready to explore **Montpellier Parade**.

*Montpellier Mews*

# Montpellier Parade

Even for Harrogate, the shops of **Montpellier Parade** are outstanding, both for their quality and range. Montpellier Parade, built in the early 1860s, was the first development carried out by the greatest of 19th century Harrogate's speculating builders, George Dawson, who went on to build some of its most impressive commercial and residential properties.

**Montpellier Parade** winds up the hill, passing several top quality shops and galleries; a good, traditional café, the **Catwalk Café**; a town centre pub, the **Montpellier**; the **Slug & Lettuce** café-bar; and **Petit Point**, specialists in needle craft, whose displays attract a large and discerning clientele.

Montpellier Parade has two further wine-bars, half way up the steep section of Montpellier Parade: **Hedley's**, one of the first, and best, in the town, and the neighbouring **Blues Bar**, a fashionable locale much frequented by a young clientele.

## Sweet reward

No visitor should miss the historic **Farrah's Harrogate Toffee Shop**. This delectable sweet-meat was invented in 1837, to take away the taste of some of Harrogate's stronger mineral waters! Don't – on any account – miss the dazzling interior displays, which include chocolates, teas, coffees and other scrumptious fare.

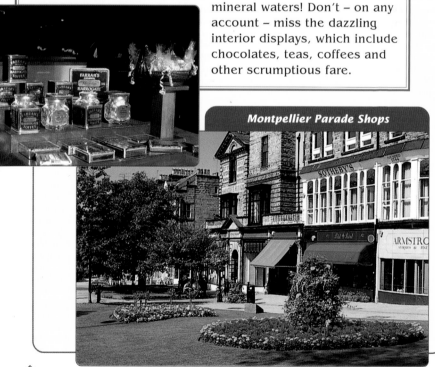

*Montpellier Parade Shops*

# Betty's Café

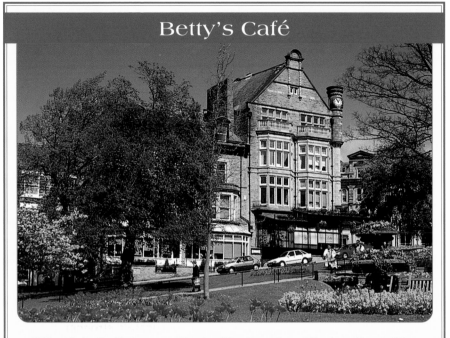

**B** etty's Café Crowns Montpellier Parade, at its junction with busy Parliament Street. Betty's is an old Harrogate institution, being justly celebrated for its superb range of teas, coffees and cakes. To sit in its pleasant tea rooms, and look out on life in Montpellier Gardens, is as diverting an occupation as any in Harrogate. Celebrities are often seen in Betty's, although since his death in 1996, James Alfred Wight – better known to millions as James Herriot – sadly, is no longer a 'regular'.

## Around Parliament Street

This busy shopping street runs from the War Memorial downhill to Crescent Gardens, and contains a good mixture of private shops, multiple retailers, pubs, wine bars and fast-food outlets.

Walking downhill, on Betty's side of the street, the visitor will encounter **Yate's Wine Lodge**, formerly the old Somerset Hotel,

frequented by a representative cross-section of the public. Popular during shopping hours with business people, families, or older shoppers, its character changes in the evening, being the haunt of a younger element of society, when 'bouncers' appear on the front steps.

Next door is the new and promising **Hogshead**, expensively reconstructed in 1998-9 as a wine-bar and pub, of which the author has – as yet – no experience.

## The Ginnel

Parliament Street is breached by the Ginnel, which leads down to Montpellier Gardens, already described. The striking building half way down the Ginnel, on the left, faced with white Scarborough Brick, is the **Harrogate Antique Centre**, an enterprising and fascinating antique market shared by several dozen businesses. Browsers can also take advantage of a delightful first floor café.

The Ginnel also contains several upmarket and attractive businesses, such as the atmospheric premises of central Harrogate's best wine merchant, **Martinez Fine Wines**, located in Exchange Cellars. Perhaps the best recommendation for Martinez is that the expert and helpful staff advise both amateur and connoisseur customers with equal deference and skill.

Next door to Martinez, **Montey's Rock Café**, a recently established flair bar, is rapidly becoming one of Harrogate's most fashionable evening spots, which opens at 17.00.

And if you don't know what a flair bar is, keep an eye on the bar attendant!

*Betty's and Upper Parliament Street*

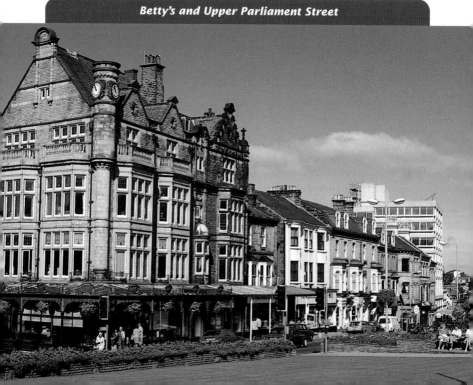

Further down Parliament Street, beyond the Ginnel crossing, a popular pub, **The Alderman Fortune** may be found, being named after Alderman Charles Fortune, one of Victorian Harrogate's greatest public figures. Beyond the pub is the entrance to the **Winter Gardens** area of the Royal Baths

The opposite side of Parliament Street, near the crown of the hill, is home to **Fattorini**, Harrogate's oldest jewellers, which was established in 1831 on High Harrogate's Regent Parade. Still a family business, Fattorini continues the tradition of selling goods of the highest quality and beauty.

The neighbouring **Maturi**, a superb gift and leather goods shop, include in their premises the former Nicholson's music shop, frequented by James A. Wight, alias James Herriot, who extended his knowledge and love of music by means of weekly visits and discussions with owner Joseph Nicholson. The music business has long closed, but **Maturi** continues to display an impressive range of stock.

Walking down Parliament Street, the junction with Oxford Street is marked by **Lloyd's Number One** café-wine bar, opposite which rises the red brick building of Parliament Street's largest department store, **Debenhams**, with five floors for retailing.

## Westminster Arcade

Lower Parliament Street is dominated on the east by the flamboyant gothic tower of the **Westminster Arcade**, built in 1898. Recent cleaning has revealed a wealth of elaborate carving, and the whole would not be out of place in Gotham City! The arcade contains two levels of fascinating speciality shops and galleries, eminently worth the visitor's attention. Beyond the Westminster Arcade may be found several exclusive high-fashion retailers, such as **Rita Valpiani**, which cater to a discerning female clientele.

**Brown's**, Harrogate's premier glass and china specialist, displays windows which are a continual delight to the passer-by. Fashion conscious males should not miss **Rhodes Wood Clothiers**, the exclusive shirt makers, at the junction of Parliament Street and Kings Road. Beyond, in Kings Road, the premises of **Goldsmiths**, jewellers and clock-makers, are recommended with confidence.

**Westminster Arcade**

# • CENTRAL HARROGATE •

**B**efore 1860, central Harrogate consisted of a few isolated houses set amidst farming fields, and criss-crossed by footpaths between High and Low Harrogate. The two principal roads were either the modern Kings and Skipton Roads, which lie to the north of central Harrogate; or, Leeds Road and York Place, to the south.

Today, the visitor can see most of the streets which now form **Central Harrogate** from the **Cenotaph**, or **War Memorial**, in **Prospect Square** at the top of Parliament Street.

## The crescents

Central Harrogate's most imposing architectural features are the two great crescents built between 1867 and 1880 by Alderman George Dawson, & designed by Hirst of Bristol : **Cambridge Crescent & Prospect Crescent.**

These are home to a number of banks, building societies and prestigious shops, such as the famous **Allens**, established in 1880 as an outfitter to the gentry.

The central open space was once the garden of the Prospect – now Imperial – Hotel. Cambridge Crescent is continued up to the junction with Oxford Street by the short **Cambridge Road**, dominated by the great tower of St Peter's Church. Here may be found the main Harrogate **Post Office**, and the long established town centre **Cambridge** café.

## The War Memorial

**T**he Cenotaph, or **War Memorial**, unveiled by the 6th Earl of Harewood in 1923, and re-dedicated after the Second World War, commemorates the sons and daughters of Harrogate who gave their lives in two World Wars. The annual November Act of Remembrance, at which the Mayor and Corporation preside, is a significant and moving event.

Designed by Prestwich & Sons, the Cenotaph takes the form of a restrained obelisk – reminiscent of the Washington Monument – being decorated with two sculpted relief panels by Gilbert Ledward.

## Retail area

Four important shopping streets radiate from Prospect Square: James Street, Cambridge Street, Oxford Street, and Parliament Street, the first three being parallel to each other.

James Street, traditionally, the Bond Street of central Harrogate, contains exclusive and up-market shops, as well as banks such as Barclays, TSB and the Yorkshire. At the time of writing, James Street is still open to vehicular traffic. Visitors should nevertheless brave the noxious traffic fumes and unsightly rows of parked cars, to inspect the exclusive fashion shops and **Hooper's Department Store**, the best such in Harrogate.

Here too is the famous **Preston's Photographic** shop, which contains a fascinating permanent display of historic cameras and provides the photographer with flawless service and skilled advice.

**Hammick's Bookstore**, beyond the elegant neo-classical Yorkshire Bank, contains what is possibly Harrogate's largest retail space for new books, housed in a fine terrace of polychrome brick and stone, designed in the 1860s by Hirst of Bristol.

## Ogdens

No visitor to James Street should fail to take in **Ogdens** the jewellers, at No.38, the beautiful Edwardian frontage of which is one of the sights of Harrogate, especially in summer, when its elegant glazed canopy is festooned with hanging flower baskets.

Founded in 1893 by J.R. Ogden, the firm – long famous for its impeccable service – has supplied items to both Winston Churchill and Mrs. Franklin D. Roosevelt.

Ogdens is one of Harrogate's oldest and best businesses.

*Victoria Shopping Centre and Gardens*

Towards the east, James Street terminates at Station Parade. Half way along the south side of James Street, **Princes Street** runs up to Princes Square and Victoria Avenue, and contains several high quality businesses, of which two may be highlighted: the popular café-bar **Raison D'etre**, whose windows can be removed in warm summer weather, and, almost opposite, **Porter's**, a specialist in high quality leather luggage and bags.

## Around Cambridge Street

**Cambridge Street**, like its neighbour, James Street, also runs from Prospect Square to Station Parade, beginning at the great church of **St Peter's**, built between 1870 & 1926 as the principal Anglican church of central Harrogate. Flanking the pedestrianised Cambridge Street, many of Harrogate's largest chain stores may be found here, including **Boots** the chemists, opposite St Peter's, housed in an elegant neo-classical stone structure.

Here too, may be found Littlewoods, Woolworth's, and British Home Stores, and, near Station Parade, the monstrous **Marks and Spencer** store, completed in 1998 in the neo-banal style of architecture.

Contrast this, with the elegant Palladian frontage of the **Victoria Shopping Centre**, built from 1990-1992 by the eminent British architect David Cullearn on the site at the corner of Cambridge Street, Station Parade and Station Square. Inspired by Palladio's famous Basilica at Vicenza, David Cullearn employed elements of the same timeless architectural language as had been used by earlier generations of Harrogate architects, but in a manner which catered to the needs of modern times.

The Victoria Centre's four floors contain a fine variety of shops, some being familiar multiple names, such as **W H Smith**, others being of a more specialist nature. Whatever the shopper's taste, the centre is well worth exploring, and the author takes pleasure in recommending the cheerful ground floor licensed continental café, **Le Soleil**, to all visitors.

## Oxford Street

Oxford Street, originally an ancient foot route between Low and High Harrogate, runs from the busy Parliament Street to the former Grand Opera House, now the Theatre. In 1999 began the conversion of eastern Oxford Street from an experimental traffic-free zone into a permanent pedestrian precinct. The design incorporates theatrical motives into the street decoration.

**Walker's Bookshop** is located above the fascinating **Good Cook's shop**, the two businesses being among the best in Harrogate. A welcoming café may be found on the first floor. Next door, in a good Victorian building restored in 1999, is **Jesper's Stationery Shop**, a long established Harrogate business, stocking an impressive range of stationery. Here, the late James Herriot, the alias of James A.

## Harrogate Theatre

The eastern entrance to Oxford Street is framed by the red brick **Harrogate Theatre**, built in 1900 as the Harrogate Grand Opera House. The plain exterior of the Theatre encloses a gorgeously elaborate Victorian interior, in which a fine standard of theatrical productions is maintained. In the entrance hall, the superb and unusual art nouveau frieze should not be missed.

The production policy is to provide a wide range of theatrical experience, including in-house, toured-in shows, cabaret reviews, stand up comedy, music recitals, dance, and the occasional children's event. The annual pantomime is an established part of the Harrogate calendar.

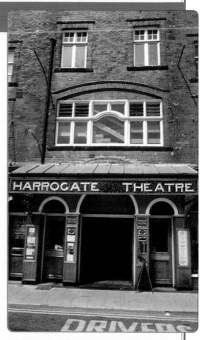

Wight, purchased his writing paper – and later his word processor!

The western section of Oxford Street, between the junctions of Cheltenham Crescent and Parliament Street, contains the great classical temple that is **Wesley Chapel**, the principal place of worship for the Methodist Congregation of central Harrogate. Built in 1862, Wesley Chapel operates an enterprising policy of encouraging visitors into its impressive building by means of regular coffee mornings, and first rate concerts, in addition to regular religious services.

## Cheltenham Crescent

Once a pleasant, tree-lined street of terrace houses, Cheltenham Crescent, together with its neighbour, Cheltenham Parade, formed a residential area which had been developed after 1870. After the Second World War, both streets became increasingly commercial, a trend which was given considerable impetus in 1981, with the opening of the Conference Centre in adjacent Kings Road.

Both streets contain several excellent shops and restaurants, of which **Est Est Est** Italian restaurant – now under new management – may be recommended with confidence. For those with a taste for Chinese cuisine, **Horoscope**, at no.1 Cheltenham Crescent (just behind Wesley Chapel) provides first rate fare and service, the shredded duck being a particularly toothsome favourite of the author.

## Antiquarian bookshop

Nearly opposite Est Est Est, on Cheltenham Crescent, and a few premises behind Wesley Chapel, **Richard Axe's Bookshop** contains the town's finest selection of out-of-print and antiquarian books, run by staff who are both efficient and friendly. This business can rival the best in London and York.

Opposite Axe's bookshop, Cheltenham Mount is home to **McTague of Harrogate**, a specialist dealer in fine prints, engravings and maps, whose display rooms are a delight to the eye, and whose business is an embellishment to the whole town.

At 17 Cheltenham Crescent, further down the hill from Richard Axe's bookshop, the

## Empire Buildings

Returning to Cheltenham Parade, and ascending the hill past the interesting premises of **Masai Mara ltd**, retail African artefacts, and the popular **Harrogate Brasserie Hotel**, identifiable by its splendid entrance canopy of cast-iron and stained glass, the junction with Mount Parade is reached. Here, the visitor will arrive at Empire Buildings, home of **Pinocchio's Restaurant**. The staff,

long established **Cattlemen's Association** Restaurant is to be found. Here, visitors may be sure of enjoying traditional steaks, including some with extremely generous portions.

The junction of Cheltenham Parade and Oxford Street, opposite Pinocchio's, is also the meeting point of two interesting shopping streets, Commercial Street, to the north, and Beulah Street, to the south. The former, **Commercial Street,** is still open to vehicular traffic, and contains many smaller shops, some of which are specialist retailers

**The Cheese Board,** Harrogate's finest cheese-monger, sells a great variety of cheese, including such Yorkshire delicacies as Blue Wensleydale and the incomparable Swaledale. Further down Commercial Street, the old established family business of **Blackburn and Swallow** sells household electrical equipment.

largely Italian, are wonderful with children, and the restaurant's cuisine is recommended with enthusiasm.

The Empire Buildings were built in 1872 as a Primitive Methodist Chapel but converted in 1911 into a Music Hall. Pinocchio's still contains many features from its Music Hall days, including a gallery and a gorgeously hand-carved proscenium arch. One of the sights of Harrogate.

# Quieter shopping

Running parallel with Commercial Street, lower Station Parade is somewhat on the fringe of the central Harrogate shopping area, but nevertheless worth investigating by the inveterate shopper, not least because it is home to the **Wild Ginger Vegetarian Bistro** – at 5 Station Parade. In 1998 this was voted, by readers of *Vegan Magazine*, best restaurant catering to vegans.

Further up, near the junction with Oxford Street, at No.20a Station Parade, may be found one of the most useful offices in Harrogate – **Harrogate & District Travel Ltd,** where information, timetables and tickets may be obtained for local bus services. The company is also an agent for the National Express Coach services. The staff are polite and helpful. At busy periods, customers may have to queue.

Opposite the top of Commercial Street, the **Beulah Street** precinct is marked by a pretty arch of ornamental iron-work. Pedestrianised in 1998, Beulah Street contains a wealth of smaller specialist shops, including **I'Anson,** a long established jewellers; **Camomile Lawn,** with its fascinating range of Indian artefacts and furniture; the lively and deservedly popular **Café Rouge,** and, housed in a splendidly flamboyant red brick and stone arcade of 1902, **Argos Sports Intersport,** a well stocked dealer in sportswear and equipment.

The pavement inscription opposite Argos sports gives a

clue to the origin of the unusual name of Beulah Street. The top of Beulah Street is marked by the junction with Cambridge Street and the Victoria Centre.

## Public transport termini

Instead of turning right into Cambridge Street, the visitor taking the left turn will arrive in the busy **Station Parade**, which forms, along with King's Road and York Place, part of Harrogate's inner ring road, itself a relic from a barbarous traffic management plan of c1970.

At the time of writing, the site across Station Parade remains un-developed. This was the traditional site of Harrogate's splendidly convenient central **Bus Station**, the location of which, next door to the Railway Station and Taxi Ranks, made Harrogate the envy of less well-planned communities.

At the time of the de-regulation of the National Bus Company, the premises were snapped up by a property developer and demolished. The present wasteland is, perhaps, an appropriate memorial to the antisocial government policy of those times. Buses still run from the truncated site.

**Copthall Tower**, which covers the Harrogate **Railway Station**, is an even bigger monument to past planning folly, being probably the most hated building in Harrogate, and consisting of a crass tower block of pre-cast panels, completed in 1965, and wholly out of keeping with anything in the town.

Turning away from this horror, **Station Square** may be seen to the west of Station Parade, framed by the Victoria Centre, and the head of James Street, at which stands the imposing bulk of the former **Station Hotel**, erected in 1873 with superb stonework.

## Memorial to Queen Victoria

Opposite, in Victoria Gardens, stands the **Queen Victoria Jubilee Monument**, erected in 1887 as a gift from the Mayor, the great Richard Ellis, to commemorate the Queen's Golden Jubilee. The statue, by Webber, is contained within an ornate gothic canopy of stone and marble.

Continuing in a southerly direction along Station Parade, as far as Station Bridge, the visitor may wish to take a two-minute walk across the shop-lined bridge to view the Harrogate **Odeon Cinema**, at the top of East Parade. This fine example of art deco architecture is of particular interest, having been designed by Harry Weedon, who was architect to the Odeon Group of Cinemas in the 1930s. Weedon was a local man, whose Harrogate design featured on the 1996 19p postage stamp.

## Return to Prospect Place

Walking back to Station Parade, the stately block of **Prince Consort Row** may be seen between Station Bridge and Victoria Avenue, fronted with a splendid canopy of decorative iron and glass. This is home to a number of interesting retail premises, the quality of which may be judged by their readiness in summer to contribute pretty hanging baskets for the embellishment of the canopy.

Crossing the busy Station Parade by one of the two neighbouring crossings, the visitor will arrive at **Sunwin House,** formerly the Co-operative, housed in an ugly 1950's shoebox of a building, on a site between the pretty Library Gardens and Albert Street. Sunwin House is one of the few big general stores left in central Harrogate, and is definitely worth the visitor's attention.

**Albert Street,** running due west from Station Parade as far as Prospect Place, has since the 1990s specialised in two activities – estate agencies; and the restaurant and wine bar business. The **Pizza Express** is a good example of the latter, being acclaimed nationally for its quality. Personally, the author considers that most pizza resembles carpet underlay, but admits to being pleasantly surprised by the pizza served at Pizza Express.

Near the western extremity of Albert Street, **John Street** runs along to James Street, containing three popular Wine Bars, **The Pitcher & Piano, Merchant Stores,** and **Via Vita** together with

## Fine linens

Prince Consort Row is home to one of Harrogate's oldest and most famous institutions – **Woods Linens.** Established in 1895, Woods Linens is probably the last remaining (and certainly the finest) linen shop in England, which also provides a unique service of interior decoration. This wonderful business represents the best of the old Harrogate tradition of top quality service and customer care. If you do not like Woods, then you may as well leave Harrogate.

a number of interesting, small, speciality shops.

Much of central Harrogate's retailing occurs in streets laid out after 1860 by the Victoria Park Company. The grandest of these is Victoria Avenue, but before this is considered, the visitor should not fail to walk along Prospect Place as far as the Prince of Wales roundabout, to the south. This is the old turnpike road between Ripon and Leeds, along which a number of hostelries were established in the early 19th century.

## West Park

Starting by the **Cenotaph**, or War memorial, the first building to be encountered is the **Imperial Hotel**, which has its origin in a lodging house opened in 1814. Beyond this, a number of handsome private houses lead to the former **Alexandra Hotel**, of 1901, at the corner of Albert Street, named after the Consort of King Edward VII, but since the 1970s subjected to a series of increasingly bizarre names.

Next to Cathcart House, the fine tower of the **West Park United Reformed Church** marks the beginning of Victoria Avenue (see below). Continuing along **West Park**, note the fine Regency Terrace of private houses, set well back from the pavement.

The point where the building line comes forward to meet the public pavement, marks the start of an interesting mixture of traditional pubs and exclusive fashion shops, shortly beyond which, at left, branches Tower Street and its multi-storey car park.

Tower Street contains the **Tap & Spile**, a fine example of a traditional English pub, special-

## Cathcart House

Beyond Albert Street may be seen the handsome Georgian styled terrace of formerly private houses, now containing the **Harrogate Spa Hotel.** Cathcart House, the single mansion between this hotel and the neighbouring church, is of special interest.

**Cathcart House** has been immortalised as Mexborough Hall by A A Thompson, in his poignant novel *The Exquisite Burden*, a story of a boy growing up in pre-First World War Harrogate.

Cathcart House, in real life, was also the favoured lodging of Princess Alix, a regular Harrogate visitor before her marriage to the Tsar of Russia. The twins born in 1894 to Mr & Mrs Allen, the then owners of Cathcart House, were adopted by Princess Alix as her godchildren, and she maintained contact with them until her murder by the Bolsheviks in 1918.

Today, the building accommodates a number of secure apartments, and is not open to the public.

*The Stray in autumn*

ising in locally brewed beers, and, across the road, the popular **U.K. Superbowl – 10 pin bowling**, which caters to a clientele of all ages.

Beyond the Tower Street junction, West Park contains two more traditional English pubs – the **Coach & Horses**, and the **West Park Hotel**. Further on lie the premises of **Ottaway's of Harrogate & Casa Fina**, an interior design and home furnishing business whose eye-catching windows are a continual delight. Within, on the first floor, the **Tent Room** restaurant provides superb views of West Park Stray.

West Park ends at the Leeds Road roundabout, dominated by the massive bulk of Prince of Wales Mansions – a former hotel, where the Wordsworths stayed in 1823. Looking across the Stray to the south-east, the imposing spire of **Trinity Church** (1879) may be seen, behind which is the **West End Park** estate, also known as the 'Oval', a model layout of impressive late-Victorian mansions built around a sequence of once-private gardens.

## Around York Place

From Prince of Wales Mansions, the street frontage now runs due east along **York Place**, as far as High Harrogate (see below), consisting of handsome Georgian and Victorian terraces and detached mansions, which between them sum up most of the 19th century's range of residential architectural styles.

A pleasant diversion may be taken by crossing the busy York

Place from Prince of Wales Mansions to the grassy expanse of **South Stray**. The curving line of ancient chestnut trees brings the visitor to the most historic Spa location in England – the **Tewit Well**.

Returning to York Place from Tewit Well (named after the Tewits, or Pewits, which gathered to peck the salt globules formed in the once open well) along the cherry tree-lined **Milton Way**, continue along **York Place** as far as **Queen Parade**. This is a dignified street, which – despite some additions of the 1960s-70s – still includes substantial stone villas, built between 1850 and 1880.

## Around Victoria Avenue

Half way down Queen Parade, there is a junction with **Victoria Avenue**, marked by an ancient oak tree, survivor from the days of the Royal Forest. Victoria Avenue was built as a show street for the Victoria Park Company, after 1860, as part of their plan to link together the two ancient villages of High and Low Harrogate to form a modern Victorian town. With its broad pavements, tree-lined grass verges, and dignified buildings, Victoria Avenue is the epitome of 19th-century town planning.

## Tewit Well – the first 'spa'

The elegant little domed temple, supported by columns in the Tuscan order, marks the location of a chalybeate (iron) spring, discovered by William Slingsby in 1571, which was the first medicinal spring in England to have the name of 'Spa' attached to it. The discovery of this Well, and its subsequent exploitation by the doctors, began Harrogate's development into a health resort.

**Milton Way**

Walking due west from the old oak tree, the south side contains the **Christian Science Church**, a neo-classical building of 1924, next to which is the **Harrogate Club**, with magnificent bay windows which admit light to the institution's great public rooms. Here, Sir Arthur Conan Doyle attended seances. Opposite, at the beautifully maintained Victoria Circus, is the **Baptist Church**, in the Decorated style, a noble building of 1883.

Continue down Victoria Avenue, and crossing the busy Station Parade at the appointed place, the **Library Gardens** are reached. This was originally the site for a great Municipal Palace, or Town Hall, of which only part – the Library – was ever built.

The **Library** of 1907, financed by the generosity of Andrew Carnegie, still bears on its east façade key-stones designed to take the rest of a much larger structure, abandoned at the time of the First World War. Currently administered by the North Yorkshire County Council, the Library contains a fine Reference and Information department, and local history collections.

**Victoria Avenue**, between Avenue Road and West Park, contains three further buildings of note. On the south side, **Vanderbilt Court** fills the entire plot between Victoria Avenue and Princess Square. This was the home of Harrogate's great 19th-century speculating builder, George Dawson. The basement of the Princes Square section of the building contains a popular wine bar and restaurant – **The Tannin Level.**

The junction of Victoria Avenue and West Park is formed on the south by the imposing **Belvedere**, built in an unusual Victorian-Tudor style for a banker. Sir Henry Rider Haggard, author of King Solomon's Mines, stayed at the Belvedere whilst working on his book *Rural England*.

Opposite Belvedere, the fine **United Reformed Church**, built in 1862 for the Congregationalists, provides West Park with its most memorable architectural feature. Nineteenth-century wits ascribed the singular appearance of the gargoyle portraits of Protestant Reformers, overlooking Victoria Avenue, to the fact that they were sculpted by a Roman Catholic artist!

## Almshouses

Opposite the library, Avenue Road is marked by the great square tower of **St Paul's United Reformed Church**, (formerly the Presbyterian Church), an austere building of 1885, beyond which lie the attractive ensemble of **St Peter's School**, and **Rogers' Almshouses.**

These were the 1868 gift of wealthy businessman George Rogers, intended for the accommodation of "widows or spinsters who have moved in a respectable position in life, but who have been reduced to poverty by circumstances over which they had no control".

## • HIGH HARROGATE •

**B**efore 1800, none of the foregoing – with the possible exception of the Old Sulphur Well, and the certain exception of the Tewit Well – would have interested visitors to Harrogate. Low Harrogate was a tiny, irregular village, and central Harrogate did not exist. For it was to High Harrogate that the visitors flocked.

Eclipsed by Low Harrogate in the early 19th century, High Harrogate is nonetheless worth visiting, particularly because of its architectural and spa heritage, the maturity of its trees, and the nobility of the open Stray, around which rotate its three principal thoroughfares.

The best route to explore High Harrogate is to begin at the **Cedar Court Hotel**, which may be reached on foot via Victoria Avenue, Queen Parade, and York Place, or via West Park and York Place, both being pleasant walks.

### High Harrogate 'triangle'

The Cedar Court Hotel, in Park Parade, occupies the beautiful building of the old Queen Hotel, which tradition places as Harrogate's oldest custom-built Inn, c1671. After closing in 1950, the former Queen Hotel became the administrative headquarters for the Regional Health Authority, but in 1998-9 the building was re-converted to hotel use.

*High Harrogate*

By 1800, the apexes of the High Harrogate 'triangle' were marked by three historic hotels – the Dragon, the Granby and the Queen. Although the Dragon was demolished in c1890, and the Granby is now Granby Court, a residential home, the luxurious Cedar Court Hotel in Queen Buildings continues High Harrogate's ancient tradition of high quality accommodation.

Follow Park Parade northwards, crossing the busy North Park Road, and – keeping the Stray to the right, and the building line to the left – admire the rich variety of Georgian and Victorian architecture which lines both Park Parade, and its continuation, Regent Parade.

At 10 Park Parade, the imposing **White House** hotel may be seen, housed in a mansion of c1830 which would not be out of place on the Grand Canal at Venice!

Number 20, now a private house, has an interesting history, being built in 1796 as Harrogate's first Methodist Chapel, and subsequently being the home – from 1890-1912 of the great watercolourist, Bernard Evans, whose studio was at roof top level.

Next door, across the entrance to Christ Church Oval, Park House (No.21) was the home of the last County Palatine Bishop of Durham, Dr. Van Mildert. Park House and its northern neighbours, including the old Parsonage of High Harrogate, form a delightful architectural ensemble, beyond which lies Walker's Passage – a convenient footpath back to Central and Low Harrogate – and the Georgian elegance of **Bilton House**, now the Register Office, with useful amenities for family historians.

## First shops

Beyond Bilton House, Regent Parade takes on a more commercial character, as the Stray narrows towards Devonshire Place, opposite, across the busy Skipton Road. This was where the first Harrogate shops were established during the Spa Season, which – until the coming of the railways in the 1840s – lasted from June to September. By now, the visitor will have experienced something of High Harrogate's great problem – traffic, produced by the over-loaded Knaresborough to Skipton road, otherwise, the A59.

At High Harrogate's narrowest point, the Stray continues as a thin strip as far as the railway line to York. Beyond this, to the northeast, the castellated outline of **Grove House** may be seen, built in the 17th century as an inn, and transformed in the 19th century by millionaire-inventor Samson Fox into a mansion. Grove House and its grounds are not open to the public.

## Church Square & beyond

The large building opposite Grove House, resembling a French *hôtel de ville*, is Grove Road School, built in 1897. Returning to Devonshire Place, the visitor should cross the Stray in a south-easterly direction towards Church Square, noting the large cream-painted building to the north, the former **Granby Hotel**.

Now a private residential centre, the Granby was once one of the country's most prestigious addresses, patronised by the higher aristocracy, and nicknamed in consequence the *House of Lords*. Here, Clive of India resided, Lawrence Sterne regaled the company, and Blind Jack, the Yorkshire road maker, eloped with the landlord's daughter.

**Church Square**, seemingly set in the middle of the Stray, was in being before the Stray was laid out in 1778. Today this most attractive part of High Harrogate is residential, but its origins lie in commercial buildings which catered to the visitors arriving in Harrogate by coach.

The **Old Theatre**, now called Mansfield House, being a private residence, is an especially attractive structure, dating from 1788, when it was built by the owner of the Granby Hotel as a place of entertainment for the town's visitors.

## St John's Well

Beyond Church Square, to the south-east, lies the little octagonal stone pump room for the **St John's Well**, an important mineral spring, discovered in 1631 and for long the most popular of Harrogate's chalybeate waters.

The spring's first pump room was built in 1788 by Alexander Wedderburn, England's Lord Chancellor, and interrogator of Benjamin Franklin. His Harrogate Mansion, **Wedderburn House**, still stands on the edge of South Stray, at the end of the raised carriage road which crosses the Stray from Church Square.

Directly east of the St John's Well, the huge new **District Hospital** marks the beginning of the busy Wetherby Road (A661) which leads to the magnificently equipped **Great Yorkshire Showground**. On the outskirts of town lies **Rudding Park**, a fine Regency house now a superb hotel and conference resort complete with 18-hole golf course, all set in many acres of fine parkland.

This section of Wetherby Road also includes **Stonefall Cemetery**, which has become the town's largest such amenity. Opened in

*Stonefall Gates*

1914, Stonefall was extended and remodelled in 1993 in a £720,000 scheme. The new garden of remembrance contains many features of the highest artistic merit, the entrance gates with their themes of water and falling stones, being of particular excellence. Stonefall is the resting place of almost one thousand allied airmen, from the Second World War, two-thirds of whom were Canadian. It is therefore of international significance.

Returning to High Harrogate's Church Square, the next point of interest is the fine, early English Gothic-styled **Christ Church,** High Harrogate's principal place of Anglican worship, which owes its present appearance to the major rebuilding of 1831. Standing in the peaceful southern churchyard, it is possible to imagine that Harrogate is still a sleepy little moorland village, rather than the administrative capital of a district of 150,000 people. Christ Church contains several fine memorials to visitors, who "came seeking health, but found eternal repose".

Crossing the Stray towards the Queen Buildings and the **Cedar Court Hotel,** the visitor has arrived back at the start of this circular description of High Harrogate.

# Samson Fox

**According to the song about old Harrogate:**

*Do you remember, the World's most famous Spa?*
*Do you remember, when Harrogate shone like a star?*
*Tom Coleman, the Pierrots, the Old Spa Rooms,*
*Otto Schwartz and his German Band,*
*Samson Fox and the roasting Ox,*
*And the Fireworks, oh so grand*

One of old Harrogate's most colourful characters, Samson Fox (1838-1903) provided public ox roastings on the Stray for occasions of national celebration, such as Queen Victoria's Golden and Diamond Jubilees, and the end of the South African Wars. He also installed Europe's first street lighting by Water Gas plant, in Parliament Street, his own invention, and introduced another of his inventions, the pressed steel railway bogey, into the United States, with the help of his friend, Diamond Jim Brady.

Always larger than life, the brilliant, generous Fox also paid for the building of the nation's Royal College of Music, in Prince Consort Road, London, directly opposite the Royal Albert Hall. Perhaps Fox's most important invention was the corrugated boiler flue, which, in an age of steam, provided manufacturers with a device of inestimable worth, in that it enabled steam boilers to produce more energy from a strengthened boiler flue.

# LOCAL WALKS

Harrogate is ringed with delightful walks, and the interested visitor should consult the detailed guidebooks which have been published, containing explanatory maps. The following examples are within easy reach of central Harrogate, and usually require 'sensible shoes'.

## Valley Gardens – Pinewoods – Birk Crag (Western Harrogate)

Beginning at the entrance to Valley Gardens, this circular walk is about three miles.

Walk through Valley Gardens, across Bogs Field, and climb Harlow Hill by the tarmac footpath until the little War Memorial is reached, at which point the path divides to the right into three sections. Taking the middle path, continue through the Pine Woods, crossing the busy Harlow Moor Road along the way, then passing the grassed clearing, and continuing along the footpath, as it descends towards Crag Lane, where the entrance to Harlow Carr Gardens may be found.

Turn right, and walk a few dozen yards as far as the left junction, which leads down to the **Harrogate Arms** pub, a popular location, especially in summer, when Morris dancers sometimes perform, assisted by the local beer. Continue past the Harrogate Arms, crossing the stream at the lowest point, when the path takes a very sharp turn to the right, leading through the delightful woods – mostly beech – until after about 400 yards a ringway signpost is reached. Turn right at the ringway post, and follow the path down to Oak Beck and across the footbridge. The waymarked footpath then leads through further woodland, until the top of Birk Crag is reached.

The ringway is exited by means of turning right and continuing along Crag Lane, either to the footpath at left, which crosses the fields to Cornwall Road, or, by returning through the Pine Woods along the same route which began the walk. The first footpath, across the fields, meets Cornwall Road, which runs back into Low Harrogate and the entrance to Valley Gardens.

Cornwall Road contains an interesting selection of private houses, mostly detached, as well as the buildings of the former Royal Bath Hospital, converted in 1997-8 to exclusive residential use.

# Nidd Gorge
## (Northern Harrogate)

Northern Harrogate provides walkers with the delightful Nidd Gorge footpath, including Old Bilton, the banks of the River Nidd and an abundance of wildlife. Those who do not wish to reach the Bilton Lane start of this walk by means of a lengthy hike along the traffic choked Skipton Road, and the apparently endless length of Bilton Lane, are advised to adopt the following procedure. Take a taxi or car to the junction of Bilton Lane with the dismantled railway track, where limited parking is also available. The walk is about two and a half miles from this point.

Follow the path a little way along the embankment in a north-easterly direction, before branching to the left, and following the path through Willow Wood, the eastern boundary of the allotment gardens until the abandoned viaduct across the River Nidd. The path then runs along the Harrogate side of the Nidd as far as the weir, before turning sharply to the right, up the steep embankment side, and across the fields. The track eventually becomes Milner's Lane, before descending once more to Bilton Lane, and the **Gardener's Arms** – a good traditional English pub – where, after due refreshment, a taxi may again be summoned.

## Crimple Valley and Hookstone Wood
## (Southern Harrogate)

This attractive walk contains the unusual **Living Bridge**, which spans a lake in Hookstone Woods. The bridge was designed by artist and engineer Jamie McCullough, and constructed in 1995 from banks of earth planted with willow. The bridge is unique in Europe, there being only one other example in the world.

Walkers are recommended to acquire one of the several excellent guides to this and other walks in the Harrogate District, as they provide maps with precise routes, together with details of ground conditions, hazards, etc, as well as local hostelries!

## • KNARESBOROUGH •

*(3 miles east of Harrogate)*
Within easy reach of Harrogate, Knaresborough is a mere eight minutes by railway, and is fully worth the attention of the visitor, as it possesses a number of nationally celebrated attractions, including one of England's finest gorge views, a ruined Royal Castle, and a varied and picturesque townscape.

*Knaresborough Castle*

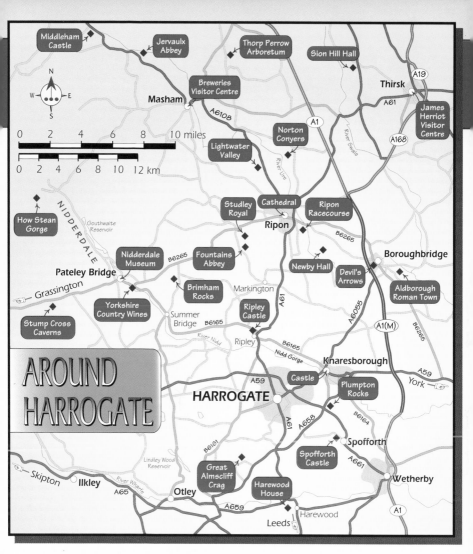

## Knaresborough Castle

If the theory of an Anglo-Saxon origin of Knaresborough is correct, then the present **Castle** can not have been the first such structure on the site. The earliest known documentary reference to the castle occurs in the Pipe Rolls for 1130, and it is likely that the first stage of building was complete by the middle of the century.

The majority of today's ruin comprises work from 1310-1340, the most visible portion of which is the great rectangular keep, which may have served as a gatehouse between the inner & outer wards. Visitors should not fail to examine the recently excavated sally-port, a subterranean passage leading from the Castle to the exterior ramparts, the steep nature of which needs to be negotiated with extreme care.

## Celebrated prisoner

The Castle dungeon retains a distinct impression of the strength and authority of the whole structure, and graffiti provides a more personal reminder of the prisoners who languished within its walls. The dungeon is probably unchanged since the time of Edward II. Perhaps the castle's most celebrated prisoner was Richard II, who lodged in the King's Chamber after being deposed by his cousin, Henry Bolingbroke, who became Henry IV.

The present ruined condition of the Castle is the result of an Act of Parliament which ordered the 'slighting', or demolition, of Royal Castles, of which Knaresborough was an important example. This was undertaken in 1648, after which the ruins were subjected to further damage by stone thieves. By the time of Turner's visit in 1826, Knaresborough Castle was a picturesque ruin.

## Exploring Knaresborough

The best place to begin an exploration of Knaresborough is at the castle, which sits high above the River Nidd, on a commanding precipice. The gorge view of the River Nidd, looking towards Harrogate, is one of the finest such views in Great Britain, the magnificent **Railway Viaduct** of 1851 being especially memorable.

Descend to the bank of the river Nidd, by the steep footpaths. Once down, the visitor may turn left and follow Waterside to the **Chapel of Our Lady of the Crag**, carved from the rock in 1408, and believed to be Britain's third oldest wayside shrine. It is guarded by a singular knight, possibly inspired by the Knights Templar of neighbouring Little Ribston.

## St Robert's Cave

Half a mile beyond the Chapel, Abbey Road leads to the site of the Priory of the Trinitarian Friars and, a further half mile brings the visitor to St Robert's Cave.

Robert Flower, born in about 1160, at York, and later known as St Robert, was a celebrated hermit, who in 1216 was visited by King John. After Robert's death in 1218, his work with the poor and imprisoned was continued by the Trinitarian Friars of the neighbouring Priory, which was founded in about 1257. Virtually nothing remains of the Priory, but its name lives on in local place names.

Retracing the path back along Waterside, via Low Bridge, the visitor will see on the opposite

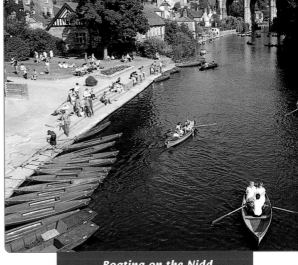

bank of the Nidd, the **Mother Shipton Inn**, one of Knaresborough's most attractive public houses.

Mother Shipton, a figure of folk-law – witch and prophetess – and one of Knaresborough's most celebrated personages, is said by some historians never even to have existed. Yet so closely is she identified with the spirit of Knaresborough, that it would be churlish to dismiss her altogether.

*Boating on the Nidd*

The earliest known reference to her appears in a publication of 1641, which associated her with York. The famous prophecies, which seemed to foretell the Great Fire of London, the Gunpowder Plot, and motor cars: *"Carriages without horses shall go, And accidents fill the world with woe"* were in truth written *after* the events they are said to describe.

Beyond the Mother Shipton Inn, on the western banks of the Nidd, lie the famous **Dropping Well** and **Mother Shipton's Cave**. The latter is an amusing curiosity, but the former is of considerable interest, being a unique petrifying well, referred to by antiquary John Leland in 1538: *"a welle of a wonderful nature callid Droping welle... what thing so ever ys caste in... and is touchid of this water, growith ynto stone"*

Visitors can still see examples of objects petrified by the water. The estate is private, the principal entrance being further along the river at High Bridge, on the Harrogate Road.

## Reminder of linen industry

Near the junction of Waterside and High Bridge, it is possible to hire boats for either rowing or punting, on the northern stretches of the Nidd. The Mill, near the dangerous weir, now in residential use, is a reminder of Knaresborough's important linen industry, which in the 18th and early-19th century produced some of the nation's finest linen.

Leaving High Bridge, the visitor should retrace their steps along Waterside, until the junction with Water Bag Bank, named after the water once transported in leather bags by donkeys, just before the mighty railway viaduct.

At this point, walk up the steep path and turn towards **St John's Parish Church**, the origins of which date from the very early 12th century. Like the Castle, St John's Church is built from a handsome magnesian limestone, and is eminently worth exploring.

**Church Lane**, which leads back to Bond End, terminates with one of the few surviving Tudor buildings in Knaresborough, the delightful **St John's House**, which dates from the last decade of the 15th century.

## Bygone Knaresborough

From St John's Church, **Kirkgate** leads up past the Railway Station, to the entrance to Castle Yard. This fine street, together with its various off-shoots, provides the visitor with a splendid impression of bygone Knaresborough. The lower section comprises mostly private residential properties, but the upper part includes shops.

At the **Railway Station**, a pretty, Victorian structure, several shops have been introduced to the platform area. Here too may be found a small but excellent restaurant, **Off the Rails**, which is the author's favourite eating place in Knaresborough. At the top of Kirkgate, the visitor should turn left, and enter the delightful Market Place.

**The Market Place**, site of Knaresborough's historic market, is a broadly rectangular space, surrounded with a variety of attractive buildings, including the former **Town Hall**. Built in 1862 in a restrained classical style, this now incorporates an attractive arcade of speciality shops.

On the opposite side of the square lies the famous **Oldest Chemist's Shop** in England, believed to have been in continuous use as a pharmacy since c1720. Following closure in 1998, the premises were rescued by Knaresborough shopkeeper Nigel Wilson, who sells vegetables alongside a museum of the apothecary's art. The arcade beneath the former Town Hall brings the visitor back to Castle Yard.

The Castle is fringed with pretty gardens, including a bowling green, beyond which rise the low buildings of the former Court House, now Knaresborough's public **Art Gallery and Museum**, established in 1977.

# • SPOFFORTH •

### *(3 miles south-east of Harrogate)*

**A**n attractive Yorkshire Village on the A661 road, and about five miles south of Knaresborough. **All Saints Church**, externally of Norman revival (1855) appearance, contains several early fragments, including some late Norman work, and a fragment of an Anglo-Saxon cross shaft, probably ninth century.

The nearby **Old Rectory** appears wholly Georgian, but the two-arched gateway is obviously of medieval origin.

## Spofforth Castle

Older than the splendidly intact Markenfield Hall, the ruined **Spofforth Castle** was actually a fortified manor house, for which Henry Percy was granted a Crenellation licence in1308.

One curious feature of this great ruin is that its back leans against a face of solid rock, so that the doorway led straight into the upper floor's great hall. From the undercroft, it is possible to inspect many interesting architectural features.

**Spofforth Castle**

## • RIPLEY & AROUND •

*(Ripley lies 2 miles north of Harogate)*

### Ripley Castle

Featuring regularly on cinema and television films, **Ripley Castle**, with its massive tower, forbidding walls, and picturesque surroundings, is everyone's ideal of what a proper castle should be. Add to this the fact that it is still a family home, a home filled with objects of interest and beauty, occupied by the same Ingilby family who have been Lords of the Manor of Ripley since about 1320, and the visitor will understand why Ripley Castle is one of Harrogate District's top attractions.

## The Ingilby family

Sir Thomas Ingilby (1290–1369) is regarded as the founder of the modern family. In 1355, during a wild boar hunt in the surrounding Royal Forest, in the company of King Edward III, Thomas Ingilby saved the King from injury and possible death by an enraged boar, and was in consequence knighted. The present baronet, also Sir Thomas, was born in 1955, and has successfully restored much of the castle and its estate.

Visitors are recommended to obtain the official guide to Ripley Castle, which has a long and fascinating history. The castle site has probably been occupied longer than the age of the oldest surviving building, which is the mid-15th century crenellated gatehouse, which stands a little to the west of the Market Place.

The greater part of Ripley Castle was constructed over two periods: 1548–55, when the three-storeyed, semi-fortified tower was raised; and 1783–86 when the buildings were remodelled by architect John Carr of York. Internally, the Knight's Chamber, the Tower Room and the Library are of especial merit, and a good story is told of Oliver Cromwell's sojourn in this last apartment.

# Ripley Village

Ripley Village owes its delightful appearance to Sir William Amcotts Ingilby (1783–1854) who, having admired a village in Alsace-Lorraine, rebuilt the whole of Ripley Village in like manner, adopting picturesque neo-Tudor and neo-Gothic styles.

This occurred in the mid-1820s, and it was also Sir William who transformed the Castle's landscape by creating the great lakes. One of Sir William's final projects was to provide Ripley with a splendid Town Hall, or *Hôtel de Ville*, the handsome Gothic style of which makes it a landmark.

Bullet holes made by Civil War troops in July 1644, can still be seen in the walls of **All Saints Church**. This attractive building was probably rebuilt after a landslide of c1395, although the upper section of the tower dates from 1567.

Vistors to Ripley may take refreshment at the **Boar's Head Hotel**, awarded the title of Yorkshire's Hotel of the year, in 1997.

The **Hob Green Hotel and Restaurant**, at Markington, just north of Ripley, midway between Harrogate and Ripon, is one of the best country restaurants in which the author has ever dined. The pretty Georgian house is set amidst 870 acres of magnificent countryside, which can be seen to advantage from the restaurant. Cattle are kept at a distance by means of a cunningly placed Ha-Ha! An altogether superior establishment.

## • FOUNTAINS ABBEY & STUDLEY ROYAL •

### *(2 miles south-west of Ripon)*

## Origins & History

First, a few facts. **Fountains Abbey,** built in a remote and heavily wooded valley, on the banks of the river Skell, was erected by monks from the Benedictine Abbey of St Mary's at York. In 1132, being dissatisfied with the laxity at St Mary's, these monks departed York to *"...a place remote from all the world, uninhabited, set with thorns... fit more, it seemed, for the dens of wild beasts than for the uses of mankind".*

The following year, the monks adopted the rules of the Cistercian order, and began to construct an abbey, which over the following centuries grew into one of the glories of the world. At the time of the dissolution of the monasteries in 1539, the great abbey church formed part of an amazing complex of buildings, which included cloisters, refectories, guest houses, warming rooms, dormitories, and an infirmary. After the dissolution, came neglect, depredation and collapse, which produced the present state of ruin. These then, are the facts.

## Author's instructions on first visit
## (if ignored, you do not deserve to return)

Knowledge of the facts of Fountains Abbey's history, is woefully inadequate as a means of preparing for the overwhelming experience which this place can give to a receptive visitor. The worst possible means of experiencing this phenomenal World Heritage Site is to stumble about its mighty ruins, guide book and map in hand, attempting to identify which section was the kitchen, which the undercroft, or which piece of wall shows 12th century work, which section reveals 16th century work.

Approach Fountains Abbey with the mind clear and calm. Note the wonderful beauty of the valley location, the flanking presence of noble trees, the surrounding meadow, the bubbling River Skell. Note, too, the acoustic of the place, the tone of bird song, the colour of the stones, and how they change in sun or rain.

**Great Cellar, Fountains Abbey**

The whole group of buildings is dominated by Abbot Huby's massive tower, built in the Abbey's twilight years, shortly before the dissolution. Within, the visitor who has approached from the gatehouse and meadow, will first find the great cellar, over 300 feet in length, above which was the lay-brothers infirmary. Beyond, to the east, lies the cloister, from which arcades – probably wooden – have long since vanished.

Here, where monks once took their exercise, audiences may now enjoy such special theatrical events as Shakespearean drama, mounted during summer months by travelling groups of professional actors. To experience *Midsummer Night's Dream*, *As you like it, or Winter's Tale*, in this setting, with rooks wheeling and cawing above, and visits by the occasional bat, is truly unforgettable.

The great Abbey church lies to the north of the monastic quarters. Having a length of 360 feet, the church contains a wealth of architectural detail, including an impressive eleven bay nave, the piers of which are surprisingly Romanesque, and completely English.

> **The author knows of no location with so distinct an atmosphere as Fountains Abbey, and if the traveller should experience only one place in England, this is it.**

## Studley Royal

The estate of **Studley Royal**, which adjoins that of Fountains Abbey, was laid out by John Aislabie, during his retirement after 1720. His son, William, in 1768, added neighbouring Fountains Abbey to the estate, thus creating one of England's most picturesque properties.

During the subsequent landscaping, meadows were formed around the Abbey ruins, and a number of delightful water features and follies constructed, including the Moon Pool, the Temple of Piety, and the Octagonal Temple.

## Studley Park

The best way to approach **Studley Park** is from the road, driving up through the deer park, towards the spired church. The great house, which possessed little architectural merit, was burned down in 1945, but the Palladian stable block, built c1716–20 on an impressive square ground plan, is still visible to the right of the main entrance drive leading up to the Church. Restored as a private house, the building is not open to public inspection.

Placed, magnificently, on a high point of vantage, **St Mary's Church** is a treasury of sumptuous alabaster, marble and stained glass, and has been described as *"one of the most perfect churches in the kingdom"*.

It was built from 1871–8 by the brilliant William Burges for the Marchioness of Ripon, being crowned with a stunning tower and spire. Although the whole church is clearly inspired by the Early-English style, it is thoroughly High Victorian in execution, and none the worse for that.

## • RIPON & AROUND •

### *(Ripon lies 12 miles north of Harrogate)*

The cathedral city of Ripon, population 14,000, is located some 12 miles from Harrogate via the A61, and within easy reach of the A1. Ripon has evidence of human settlement which pre-dates Roman times, including the largest number of earthworks and henges in the country. Some of these date from Megalithic and Bronze Age times.

The Romans, too, left their mark on Ripon, with an elaborate system of roads, passing within a few miles of the city. Indeed, 19th-century peat diggers, on the surrounding moors, unearthed the preserved body of a man wearing a toga. At the heart of the city, within the incomparable Cathedral, there is also the crypt, with the oldest known surviving post-Roman vault in England, which incorporates re-used Roman stones.

**Ripon Market Square**

# Role of the Church

The Church is to Ripon as the Castle is to Knaresborough or the Spa to Harrogate: a central theme of its history. Indeed, the very first reference to Ripon occurs in the granting, by a Northumbrian Prince, of land to a group of Celtic monks, but it was not until 1836 that it became a Cathedral city in the modern sense.

Although the names of St Wilfrid and Ripon are virtually synonymous, the saint spent little time in the city. St Wilfrid, who died in about 710, after having built the first of Ripon's cathedrals in the 670s, participated in the important River Nidd synod of 704–5. He still walks the city streets, in the form of an actor recreating the 'Wilfrid Procession', which originated back in the 13th century.

This was a religious ritual in which relics of the saint were paraded through the city. When the shrine was destroyed in the Reformation, the later reintroduction of the procession required the use of an effigy, today an actor with attendants. The procession celebrates the saint's safe return, in 686, from exile.

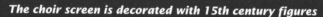

**The choir screen is decorated with 15th century figures**

# Ripon Cathedral

One of the great buildings of England, **Ripon Cathedral** has its origin in a monastery founded c657 by Alchfrith, under king of the Deirans, which was re-established a few years later by St Wilfrid, on a different site. The church and its associated monastery are thought to have been destroyed in 948, during the ravaging of Northumbria, by the English King Eadred. However, by 995, it had recovered sufficiently to shelter the remains of St Cuthbert for three months. It was during the tenth century that the establishment became a college for secular canons.

## Early building

**W**ork on the present church began c1175, when the Archbishop of York, Roger of Pont l'Eveque constructed the transepts, and part of the choir. The crypt is, however, far older, having been constructed by St Wilfrid, c670. Externally, the west front is considered to be one of the finest parts of the Cathedral, having been built in c1220–30 in a noble Early English style.

When viewed as a single structure, Ripon Cathedral may appear to be somewhat ground-hugging, but this is because the squat central crossing tower and its west front counterparts lack their spires, which provided such a powerful vertical element to the design. The spires of the crossing tower collapsed in 1615, and those of the west front were removed in 1664.

Internally, the church is intimate in scale, and contains evidence of the many changes introduced during the centuries of construction. The Chapter House and Chancel are of particular architectural merit.

# Market Square

Ripon's Market probably dates from the tenth century, the tradition of a Thursday timing resulting from the visits to Ripon of pilgrims worshipping at the shrine of St Wilfrid, who died on a Thursday. **Market Square**, Ripon's principal external place of public assembly, contains a number of interesting buildings, including the great **Obelisk**, which is the oldest free-standing obelisk in the country.

As the focal point of secular Ripon, the Market Place has always been a popular site for inns and hotels, and the grand old **Unicorn Hotel** on the south-east side, is a fine example of such establishments. The Unicorn, and the nearby **Black Bull Hotel**, were once Ripon's principal Coaching Inns.

One of Ripon's finest secular buildings, the **Town Hall** stands opposite the Obelisk, in the Market Square. Built in 1801 in a restrained but elegant Palladian style, designed by James Wyatt, the Town Hall displays the

## The Hornblower and the Bellringer

Ripon's obelisk witnesses a remarkable daily ritual at 9.00pm, with the curfew ceremony of 'setting the watch'. A hornblower, dressed in 18th century costume, sounds the traditional Ripon Horn, at each of the four corners of the obelisk, thus warning the city of the arrival of the nightly curfew.

The traditional market day bell is rung at 11.00am on Market Days, although the bellman no longer announces the sale of wives!

historic motto, *"Except Ye Lord keep Ye Cittie, Ye Wakeman Waketh in Vain"*

A near neighbour to the Town Hall, the **Wakeman's House** is an interesting, two-storeyed timber-framed building, of some antiquity.

## Beyond the Market Place

A number of interesting buildings are within easy reach of the Market Place, of which the following are particularly commended to the attention of the visitor:

Leave the Market Place via Low Skellgate and Minster Road, in the direction of the cathedral, and the late **Georgian Court House** will be reached, located behind the arch. Nearby is the former **Deanery**, a stately building with a 17th century façade.

Turn right at the Cathedral, and walk down Bedern Bank before turning left into High St Agnesgate, wherein stands the historic **Thorpe Prebend House**, whose 17th-century walls stand atop 13th-century foundations. Current plans call for the restoration of Thorpe Prebend House, in the context of a larger scheme of urban renewal.

**The Warehouse** is one of the best of Ripon's cafes, and **Primos**, a Kirkgate Italian restaurant, ideal for families, is also recommended.

## Interesting Museums

Two fascinating museums may be found in Ripon. Walking north from Market Place, via Finkle Street, Allhallowgate is reached, where stands the **Old Workhouse**, built in 1854 as a Union Workhouse, and recently restored, containing a Poor Law Museum.

If the visitor continues along Allhallowgate, turning right at the junction with St Marygate, the former Prison and 'House of Correction' is reached. This might, at first sight, be considered too grim a place for visitors, but its contents are of exceptional interest, comprising as they do the **Ripon Prison and Police Museum**, which opened here in 1984.

## Ripon Races

Ripon was once famous for the quality of its spurs, and the proverb *As true steel as Rippon Rowels* gives evidence of this. King James I, when visiting Ripon in 1617, was presented with a pair of silver spurs, with which he was reportedly delighted. Today, Ripon's connection with horses lies in the famous races, which were first run in c1714, and which are today held at the Boroughbridge Road site.

## Ripon's Waterways

Although Ripon is located between the Rivers Ure and Skell, it also has a canal, which was completed in 1773 for the purpose of linking the city to the navigable parts of the River Ure, and from there to the sea via the Rivers Ouse and Humber.

At the time of writing, it is fair to state that final restoration is still some time ahead, and that the attractiveness of Ripon's waterways consists of a number of imaginatively restored 'pockets', rather than a continuous totality, but they are worth seeing nevertheless. They are, incidentally, the most northerly point of the English canal system.

# Newby Hall

**Newby Hall**, one of the great treasure houses of England, lies across the A61 road between Ripon and Boroughbridge. Unquestionably the finest of Harrogate District's stately houses, Newby Hall's external restraint belies the lavishness of its interior.

Originally built in the 1690s by Ripon's MP, Sir Edward Blackett, the house and estate were purchased in 1748 by Richard Weddell. His son William was a great collector of art who employed architects Carr of York and Robert Adam, to create one of the finest neo-classical interiors in the country.

Newby Hall, which is the home of the Compton family, is surrounded by 25 acres of some of England's most sublime gardens.

The interior of the house has so many magnificent rooms, containing so many objects of beauty, that it would be invidious to attempt a selection. Nevertheless the attention of the visitor should be directed towards the Entrance Hall, the Regency Dining Room, the Billiards Room, the Tapestry Room, the Library, and the Statue Gallery – which last stunning room inspired the classical galleries in Washington's National Gallery of Art.

# Lightwater Valley

Situated about a mile and a half north of Ripon on the A6108 and described as a Country Theme Park, **Lightwater Valley** contains a great variety of ingenious rides which provide fun and thrills for all the family. Here, the world's longest rollercoaster ride may be experienced, together with the *Falls of Terror,* the *Bat Flyer,* the *Sewer Rat,* the *Viper,* and the *Ladybird.*

All these rides can be enjoyed after payment of a single entrance fee, which covers everything. Lightwater also encompasses a classic fairground, a circus, centres for 'fast food' and a restaurant, and a generously stocked 'factory shopping' centre. In addition, Lightwater Valley has a 175 acre woodland setting, a Forest Fort, and – a great favourite with smaller children – 'Old MacDonald's Farm'.

# Norton Conyers

This extraordinary house lies four miles to the north of Ripon, on the quiet road to Wath. The medieval origins of **Norton Conyers** are clearly visible in its fenestration, with the most striking feature being the enormous gables which were added at the time of Richard Graham during the reign of Charles II.

King Charles I stayed here in 1632, as did the future James II and his Queen, in 1679; more recently, Charlotte Brontë visited the house in 1839. It is believed that the previous century's legend of the confinement of a mad woman in the attics, provided the author with the idea for Mrs Rochester in *Jane Eyre.*

The fine park, with its 18th-century walled garden and orangery, yew hedges and herbaceous border, form a gorgeous setting for the characterful old house.

## • BOROUGHBRIDGE •

### (10 miles north-east of Harrogate)

Once a very important coaching stop on the Great North Road, Boroughbridge, some ten miles to the north-east of Harrogate, originates from the time of William the Conqueror, but is neighbour to some far older sites. The imposing Crown Hotel was once known to every coach driver between north and south, and is still a fine establishment; behind it is the large Market Square.

This pleasant open space contains an unusually large **Market Cross**, dating from 1875, and taking the form of a polygonal open-arched structure with Tuscan columns.

## Devil's Arrows

This famous prehistoric monument is to be found south-west of Boroughbridge, consisting of three impressive monoliths of millstone grit, which stand an average of 20ft above the ground. According to legend, the stones were made by the Devil's rope when he was attempting to hang his grandmother.

Less colourful is the explanation that they are part of a complex of neolithic or early bronze age ceremonial monuments, which continue north for 11 miles, and which include the henges at Cana, Hutton Moor, and Thornborough.

# • ALDBOROUGH •

*($^3/_4$ mile south-east of Boroughbridge)*
The fact that this delightful little village contains some very pretty houses, a manor house, a hall, an unusual village cross, and a superb parish church, would not, in themselves, provide sufficient reason to single out Aldborough from the area's many other villages, for inclusion in this book. Aldborough, however, contains the Roman Town of *Isurium Brigantum*, one of Yorkshire's most important Roman sites.

## Isurium Brigantum

The Brigantes, described by Roman historian Tacitus as being the largest of the British tribes, were well settled in this area at the time of the Roman occupation. The ancient township appears to originate from the first century AD, when it was a military camp of the famous Ninth Legion, which by AD150 had grown into *Isubrigantum*, the most northerly of the Roman tribal administrative centres.

The **Museum**, and its adjacent garden, contain excavated remains of the Roman settlement, including some outstanding examples of tessellated pavements, housed in little stone shrines.

## Village Cross & Church

Probably of 15th-century origins, the Village Cross consists of a shaft with a reassembled upper section, fitted together with more enthusiasm than accuracy.

Beyond, lies the beautifully maintained **Church of St Andrew**, with its solid, Perpendicular west tower. The aisles and nave date from c1360, and the interior of the church contains much of interest, including fragments of a Roman altar with a figure of Mercury.

## • PATELEY BRIDGE •

*(14 miles west of Harrogate)*
Pateley Bridge, the 'Capital of Nidderdale', is on the B6165 road beyond Ripley Village. As with Aldborough, Pateley Bridge has Roman relics, including remains of a rectangular Roman marching camp.

In Old Church Lane, a particularly steep hill, the ruins of old **St Mary's Church** come into view. The unbuttressed west tower dates from 1691. The nearby **Church of St Cuthbert**, built in 1827 by Woodhead & Hurst, has an attractive interior, where some fine late 19th-century Belgian stained glass may be seen.

No visit to Pateley Bridge is complete without taking tea in one of the many attractive cafés which line the High Street. Children can also enjoy the **Recreation Ground**, with its slides and swings, and the splendid Victorian style **Band Stand** is enjoyed by all, especially when the advertised brass band recitals are given.

Two recent attractions for visitors to Pateley Bridge are the **Nidderdale Museum** and its neighbouring **Crafts Centre**. The

## Yorkshire Country Wines

Twelve miles from Harrogate, past Ripley, Summer Bridge, and just before the B6165 runs into Pateley Bridge, the little village of Glasshouses is reached, where – delightfully situated on the banks of the River Nidd – **Yorkshire Country Wines** have their home.

Here, wines are produced from Yorkshire fruits and flowers, and the author can attest to their deliciousness and potency. Run by enterprising Richard and Gillian Brown, the premises also sell a range of interesting antiques, and provide a first rate tearoom. This is a business of which the Harrogate District can be proud.

museum provides comprehensive and convincing insight into Dales life, which won it the coveted National Heritage Museum of the Year award, in 1990.

For over one hundred years, Pateley Bridge has held a famous annual event – the **Nidderdale Show**. Every September, this fine, traditional agricultural show draws crowds to inspect the displayed livestock and country craft, which is one of the sights of Yorkshire.

The **Nidderdale Festival** of arts, crafts and music, is also an annual event, being held every June and July. This is no pale imitation of larger festivals, but an original event, which enjoys support from a wide geographical area.

## How Stean Gorge

Nicknamed 'Yorkshire's Little Switzerland', **How Stean Gorge** is an 80ft deep limestone cleft, located about 12 miles beyond Pateley Bridge in upper Nidderdale. The gorge is home to an abundance of lichens, mosses and ferns, and is spanned by three bridges of varying altitudes, which also provide a fine view of the surrounding trees.

There is also **Tom Taylor's Cave**, which gives the adventurous visitor the chance to explore a real cave. A restaurant and tearoom, with good home cooking, is also available.

*Nidderdale Museum*

# • MASHAM & AROUND •

## (22 miles north-west of Harrogate)

Masham, pronounced 'Mass-am', is a delightful village, situated about 15 miles north-east of Pateley Bridge, or 22 miles north-west of Harrogate. Masham possesses a fine, spacious market place, on which is held a lively market every Wednesday and Saturday.

Retailing has also spread into a number of atmospheric alley properties surrounding the square, which the visitor is recommended to explore. Local people are rightly proud of their famous annual sheep fair, and the Steam and Fair Organ rally.

Visitors searching for refreshment can call at 2 Church Street, the location of the **Mad Hatter Tea Shop**, which is recommended with confidence.

## St Mary's Church

Masham's architectural glory is the historic **St Mary's Church**, the fabric of which seems to exude the spirit of old Yorkshire. The lower courses of the great tower are Norman, with the upper sections dating from the 14th-century rebuilding. Above, the 15th-century octagonal belfry, with its spire, provide the Masham skyline with its most characteristic feature.

The interior possesses good Victorian and modern work, as well as relics of much earlier times. Notice should be taken of the nativity painting above the chancel's arch, attributed to Sir Joshua Reynolds. Note, too, the remarkable seven foot fragment of the shaft of an Anglo-Saxon cross, sited just outside the south porch.

## Theakston's

Robert Theakston began brewing in the Black Bull Inn at Masham back in 1827, and in 1875 his son, Thomas, built a new brewery in Paradise Field. Today, Masham is not only headquarters to the celebrated Theakston Brewery, but it is also home to the popular Theakston Visitors' Centre, which is a wonderful way to learn about brewing.

The importance of the brewing trade to Masham is well illustrated by the **Black Sheep Brewery Centre**, which opened as recently as 1992, although it looks as if it has been here for ages. There is an excellent museum and refreshment centre, and tours of the brewery last about an hour.

## Near Masham

Masham is well placed for easy access to several sites of outstanding importance, which lie beyond the boundary of the Harrogate District. These include **Thorp** **Perrow Arboretum**, the sublime ruined **Jervaulx Abbey**, **Sion Hill Hall** – with its fabulous antiques and birds of prey – and **Middleham Castle**, a favourite residence of the Percy family and of King Richard III

## Natural landmarks

In addition to the large expanses of fine countryside, the Harrogate District contains several unique natural landmarks, of which the following are particularly attractive:

- **Brimham Rocks** – about five miles east of Pateley Bridge, and probably the most singular rock formation in England.

- **Great Almscliff Crag** – about five miles south-west of Harrogate.

- **Plumpton Rocks** – about two miles south-east of Harrogate.

  All three are fantastic outcrops of climatically sculpted rock, which form dramatic additions to the landscape, and which in summer are popular picnic spots.

- **Stump Cross Caverns** – the Harrogate District's most westerly attraction. These fantastic underground caverns were discovered by Nidderdale's lead miners, and are now open to the public, who must, however, exercise the greatest care in traversing the weird subterranean spaces.

## • OTHER PLACES OF INTEREST WITHIN THE HARROGATE DISTRICT •

The Harrogate District contains a considerable variety of attractive landscape, that to the west and north-west of the town being most popular with walkers. The upper reaches of Nidderdale provide many of the finest country walks, and it is suggested that the excellent series of maps and guide books sold by the district's tourist and information offices should be consulted. The Ordnance Survey's outdoor leisure maps are recommended with particular confidence.

## Harewood House

If the boundary of the Harrogate District had been placed a further two miles south, it would have encompassed **Harewood House**, one of Europe's greatest private palaces. As it is, Harewood House and **Harewood Village** lie just across the river Wharfe, which is no reason whatsoever to exclude them, as they are only a 12-minute car or bus journey from central Harrogate.

**Harewood House** is the family home of the Lascelles family, with the 7th Earl and Countess being the current owners. The Lascelles family has been in Yorkshire from the time of the Norman Conquest, but it was not until 1739 that one of

### Harwood or Harewood!

Visitors to Harewood should note that the pronunciation of the name of the village is different from that of the house and earldom. The former is pronounced Hare-wood, whereas Har-wood is used for the latter. To complicate matters, the same spelling is used for both subjects.

their members, Henry Lascelles, acquired adjoining estates at Gawthorpe and Harewood.

Henry's son, Edwin Lascelles, built Harewood House between 1759 and 1771, to designs by Carr of York and, later, Robert Adam. On Edwin's death in 1795, the house and estate passed to his cousin, Edward, who became 1st Earl of Harewood in 1812.

It was during the lifetime of the 3rd earl, Henry Lascelles, that the house was substantially remodelled by Sir Charles Barry, architect of the Houses of Parliament, and it is Barry's work which gives the façades of Harewood House their unique and unforgettable appearance.

## Watercolour collection

Widely regarded as England's greatest painter, Turner visited Harewood in 1797. His work, together with that of John Varley and Thomas Girtin, may be seen in the so-called watercolour rooms, the Harewood collection of such watercolours being of national importance.

## Gardens and park

Much of the surrounding landscape was created by 'Capability' Brown, including the noble lake, which provides such a lovely feature to the south. The Gardens, Lakeside Walk, and Bird Garden – opened in 1970 – are additional delights.

*Opposite: Brimham Rocks*

The author has direct experience (or evidence of their excellence) of the amenities and businesses named and recommended in this guide.

## HARROGATE – HOW TO GET THERE

Once, it was only necessary to tell one's chauffeur to drive to Harrogate. Today, however, more detailed instructions may be required. Harrogate is just near enough to major airports, motorways and rail stations, to be convenient, just far enough away from these amenities to be peaceful.

### Airports

Large international airports, within easy reach of Harrogate, may be found at Manchester, about 50 miles west of Harrogate on the wrong side of the Pennines, via the busy M62 motorway; or at Tyneside Airport at Newcastle, some 70 miles north of Harrogate, via the A1 road. Best of all is the convenient and civilised Leeds-Bradford airport, some eight miles south of Harrogate. The author urges travellers to use Leeds-Bradford airport whenever possible.

### Bus and coach services

Harrogate is well served by bus services, although the central Bus Station on Station Parade operates from truncated premises, following de-regulation of the bus companies. Harrogate & District Travel run an excellent information and ticket office, at 20a Station Parade, and they are also agents for National Express bus services. The office provides timetables and sells tickets.

**Local buses** run from central Harrogate out to Boroughbridge, Knaresborough, Pateley Bridge, Ripley and Ripon, as do services to Leeds Tadcaster, Wetherby and York. Route maps identify location of bus stops, and it is the author's experience that buses are usually clean and convenient.

**National Express** bus services collect and set down passengers only at the Victoria Avenue stop, adjacent to Library Gardens. (They are not currently available from the Station Parade Bus Station.) These excellent services transport passengers between Edinburgh, London, Leeds, Chester, Newcastle, and Wrexham, etc. Travellers are advised always to check travel times in advance.

### Railways

Harrogate is connected by rail to both Leeds and York, each journey, including stops, lasting about 33 minutes. Masham, Pateley Bridge, Ripley and Ripon are not, unfortunately, connected to the railway system. Timetables and routes are freely available at the ticket and information office at Harrogate Station in Station Parade.

There is also a limited direct service to London, run by Great North Eastern Railways, which leaves Harrogate at about 7.00am, arriving at King's Cross

at about 10.00am. For passengers travelling via either Leeds or York, it is possible to reach London, or Edinburgh regularly throughout the day. All other parts of the nation's railway network may also be reached via Leeds or York, providing passengers are prepared to make the appropriate connections.

## Road links

Harrogate's two most regular road connections are the A1, which runs east of Leeds, due north. Motorists for Harrogate may either join the A661 at Wetherby, about 8 miles from Harrogate, or, they may continue along the A1 to Allerton where the busy junction with the A59 is reached, which runs westerly into Knaresborough and then Harrogate. Visitors arriving via Manchester can use the busy M62 motorway as far as Leeds, before joining the A61 which runs north through Leeds before reaching south Harrogate some 15 miles away.

## GETTING AROUND HARROGATE TOWN

The ideal way to explore Harrogate is on foot, save for the outer areas, which are best reached by bus, taxi, or private car. The disabled visitor, who requires transportation, needs to know that although some of the town's principle shopping streets – such as James Street, Parliament Street, and Station Parade – are open to vehicular traffic at all times, other important streets such Beulah Street, Cambridge Street and Oxford Street are pedestrianised, and that access to vehicular traffic is limited to specified periods. A number of dedicated disabled parking spaces are provided at key locations on the periphery of the pedestrianised area.

## Car Parking

In the town centre, the following car parks are important:

(1) **Victoria Car Park**, contiguous to the Victoria Shopping Centre and the Railway Station, and linked to each by a covered walk. This state of the art, multi-storey car park is reached via East Parade, being the first turning on the left as this road descends the hill.

(2) **East Parade Car Park**, at foot of East Parade, junction with Park View. A smaller surface car park.

(3) **Odeon Car Park**, in Station Road, behind the Odeon Cinema. A large surface car park.

(4) **Tower Street Car Parks**. These include a multi-storey car park, and a surface car park, reached from West Park. Approach via the one way traffic flow on West Park, keeping in the right lane, before turning right into Tower Street.

(5) **Union Street Car Park**. This important town centre car park is now showing its age, but is conveniently located at the heart of Harrogate's central shopping area, just off Oxford Street. Reached via Cambridge Road or Cheltenham Crescent, and eastern Oxford Street.

**On street parking** is available when parking tickets are purchased from the vending machines erected specially for this purpose.

## Taxi services

Harrogate District is well provided with taxi cabs, and of the many reliable services, the author can vouch for the following :

### Harrogate

**Airport Star Cars**
3a North Park Road, Harrogate,
☎ 01423 500515

**Bee Line Taxis**
18a King's Road, ☎ 01423 564200

**Blue Line Cars**
6 Strawberry Dale,
☎ 01423 503037

**Interline Taxis**
20 Crescent Road,
☎ 01423 564646

**Spa Taxis**
3 North Park Road,
☎ 01423 501501

**Yellow Line Taxis**
57 East Parade, ☎ 01423 521531

There are taxi ranks in James Street, and Station Parade, opposite the railway station.

### Knaresborough

**Dixieline Cars**
59 Charlton Drive,
☎ 01423 866310

### Ripon

**Radio Cars of Ripon**
Unit one, Ash Grove,
☎ 01765 692999

**Ripon City Market Taxis**
Market Place, ☎ 01765 601283

## ACCOMMODATION IN HARROGATE

## Hotels – large

**Cairn**
Ripon Road, ☎ 01423 504005

**Cedar Court** (former Queen Hotel),
Park Parade, ☎ 01423 858585

**Crown**
Crown Place, ☎ 01423 567755

**Imperial**
Prospect Place, ☎ 01423 565071

**Majestic**
Springfield Avenue,
☎ 01423 568972

**Moat House International**
King's Road, ☎ 01423 849988

**Old Swan**
Swan Road, ☎ 01423 500055

**St George**
Ripon Road, ☎ 01423 561431

## Hotels — medium or small

**Balmoral**
16 Franklin Mount,
☎ 01423 508208

**Grants**
Swan Road, ☎ 01423 560666

**Greenpark**
Valley Drive, ☎ 01423 504681

**Harrogate Brasserie**
28-30 Cheltenham Parade,
☎ 01423 505041

**Harrogate Spa**
West Park, ☎ 01423 564601

**Kimberley**
15 King's Road,
☎ 01423 505613

**Ruskin**
1 Swan Road, ☎ 01423 502045

**Studley**
28 Swan Road,
☎ 01423 560425

**White Hart**
Cold Bath Road, ☎ 01423 505681

**White House**
10 Park Parade, ☎ 01423 501388

## EATING OUT

### Cafés and Café-Restaurants

**Betty's**
1 Parliament Street,
☎ 01423 502746

**Cambridge Café**
Cambridge Road, ☎ 01423 502935

**Catwalk Café**
18 Montpellier Parade,
☎ 01423 567127

**Magnesia Well Café**
Valley Gardens, ☎ 01423 525149

**Milan's Coffee House**
47 Oxford Street, ☎ 01423 536606

**Old Coffee Shop**
39 Swan Road, ☎ 01423 507876

**Le Soleil**
(Victoria Centre), Station Square,
☎ 01423 520926

**Tent Room**
21 West Park, ☎ 01423 505871

### Pubs

It is increasingly difficult to distinguish between café-bars, wine bars, licensed restaurants and pubs. The following are good examples of traditional English pubs – whatever this may mean. The author does not frequent fake Irish "theme" pubs, hence their exclusion from this guide.

**Alderman Fortune**
51 Parliament Street,
☎ 01423 502759

**Coach & Horses**
16 West Park, ☎ 01423 568371

**Empress**
Church Square, ☎ 01423 567629

**Gardeners Arms**
Bilton Lane, ☎ 01423 506051

**Hale's Bar**
1 Crescent Road, ☎ 01423 569861

**Pine Marten**
Beckwith Knowle, Otley Road,
☎ 01423 533091

**Shepherd's Dog**
141 Otley Road, ☎ 01423 533031

**Tap & Spile**
Tower Street, ☎ 01423 526785

**Fact File**

## Restaurants

**※ more expensive　　※ modest price**

**Café Fleur ※**
3 Royal Parade, ☎ 01423 503034

**Cattlemen's Association ※**
17 Cheltenham Crescent,
☎ 01423 561456

**Drum and Monkey ※ ※**
Montpellier Gardens,
☎ 01423 502650

**Est Est Est ※**
16 Cheltenham Crescent,
☎ 01423 566453

**Lords ※ ※**
8 Montpellier Street,
☎ 01423 508762

**Millers – the Bistro ※ ※**
1 Montpellier Mews,
☎ 01423 530708

**Old Bell Tavern ※**
6 Royal Parade (re-opened 1999)
☎ 01423 507930

**Oliver's 24 ※ ※**
24 King's Road, ☎ 01423 568600

**Pinnochio's ※**
Empire Buildings, Cheltenham
Parade, ☎ 01423 560611

**Pizza Express ※**
2 Albert Street, ☎ 01423 531041

**Tannin Level ※**
5 Raglan Street, ☎ 01423 560595

**Villu Toots ※ ※**
Balmoral Hotel, Franklin Mount,
☎ 01423 705805

**William & Victoria's ※ ※**
(upstairs) 6 Cold Bath Road,
☎ 01423 521510

## Winebars

**Blues Café Bar**
4 Montpellier Parade,
☎ 01423 566881

**Christie's Wine Bar**
20 King's Road, ☎ 01423 507971

**Court's Crown Place**
1 Crown Place, ☎ 01423 536336

**Edwards**
46 Parliament Street,
☎ 01423 566576

**Hedley's Wine Bar**
5 Montpellier Parade,
☎ 01423 562468

**Lloyd's number one**
18-20 Parliament Street,
☎ 01423 538701

**Merchant Stores**
Unit 3-4, John Street,
☎ 01423 536651

**Montey's Rock Café**
The Ginnel, ☎ 01423 526652

**Pitcher & Piano Ltd**
Unit 5-6, John Street,
☎ 01423 565628

**Raison D' Etre**
5 Princes Street, ☎ 01423 725840

**Slug & Lettuce**
13a Montpellier Parade,
☎ 01423 508444

**Via Vita**
1 John Street, ☎ 01423 566333

**William & Victoria's**
(downstairs), 6 Cold Bath Road,
☎ 01423 506883

GARDENS
=======

## Harrogate town

The whole of central Harrogate takes on the appearance of a huge garden in summer, to which admission is free. Follow the white symbols on the pavements, as they are a guide to the **floral trail** (leaflet available), linking one such attraction with another.

*Crescent Gardens*
Crescent Road.

*Prospect Gardens*
Prospect Place.

*Montpellier Gardens*
Montpellier Parade.

*Harlow Carr Botanical Gardens*
The North of England Horticultural Society's gardens, at Crag Lane.
   Open every day at 9.30am, closing at 6.00pm or dusk, whichever comes first.
   Admission charges vary: (at the time of publication) Adults at £3.60; Senior Citizens at £2.70; Students at £1.80 and children up to 16 accompanied by an adult, free. ☎ 01423 565418.

*Valley Gardens*
A magnificent public park, always open, admission free, at the heart of Low Harrogate, with a main entrance at the junction of Valley Drive and Cornwall Road.

## Knaresborough

The attractive **Bebra Gardens**, within easy reach of Knaresborough's Castle, commemorate Knaresborough's twin, Bebra, in Germany. These peaceful gardens deserve to be better known, as they are a delightful oasis. Admission free.

## Ripon

The **Spa Gardens**, adjacent to the Spa Baths Swimming Pool, provide this ancient city with a fine floral centre, of which the Victorian bandstand is an especially attractive feature. Admission free.

## GUIDED TOURS OF HARROGATE

The author of this book is an expert and experienced guide to Harrogate town, and indeed assisted in the establishment and training of the voluntary guides who take pleasure in introducing the delights of Harrogate to the many visitors requiring these services – either singly, or in larger groups. Because the guides are voluntary, and provide a free service, the following timetable may, on occasion, be varied:

The season opens at Easter, and closes in late October, with the point of assembly being next to the entrance to the Royal Pump Room Museum in Crown Place. Guided walks are provided every day, except Fridays and

Saturdays, and start at 2.30pm on Sundays, Mondays and Wednesdays, and 11.00am on Tuesdays and Thursdays. They usually last for an hour.

## HARROGATE INTERNATIONAL FESTIVAL

Usually held in July and August each year, offering a full range of classical, jazz and blues music, dance, street entertainment and fringe events. For more details contact the Festival Office in Victoria Avenue on ☎ 01423 562303.

## MUSEUMS & GALLERIES
## (charges at time of publication)

### Harrogate

**Mercer Art Gallery**
Swan Road, ☎ 01423 556188.
Opening times: Tues to Sat 10am–5pm, Sun 2–5pm. Free.

**Royal Pump Room Museum**
Crown Place, ☎ 01423 556188.
Opening times: Mon to Sat 10am–5pm, Sun 2–5pm. Adults £2.00, Children and senior citizens £1.50.

**Visitor Centre at water bottling plant** (planned).

**Harlow Carr Museum of Gardening**
Crag Lane, ☎ 01423 565418.
Opening times: Daily, 10am–4pm. Adults £3.60, Senior citizens, £2.70; Students £1.80.
Accompanied child free. In winter, £1.50. Includes entry to gardens.

### Aldborough

**Isurium Brigantium Roman Town and Museum**
Opening times: April 1 to Sep 30, daily 12–5pm.
Admission: £1.40, concession £1.10, children 70p.

### Knaresborough

**Old Court House Museum and Gallery**
Castle Grounds, ☎ 01423 503340.
Opening times: Easter to end Sep, daily, 10.30am–5pm.
Admission: Adults £1.75, Senior Citizens & children £1.00.

**St Robert's Cave**
Abbey Road, ☎ 01423 503340.
Open daylight hours.
Admission free.

**Knaresborough Castle**
Castle Grounds. ☎ 01423 503340.
Opening times: Easter weekend to end of Sep, daily, 10.30am–5pm.
Admission: Adults £1.75, Senior Citizens & children £1.00.

### Pateley Bridge

**Nidderdale Museum**
King Street, ☎ 01423 711225.
Opening times: Easter to October, daily, 2–5pm. November to Easter, Sat & Sun 2–5pm; Aug 11am–5pm. Admission: Adults £1.00, Senior Citizens and children 50p.

# Ripon

### Police and Prison Museum
27 Marygate, ☎ 01765 690799
Opening times: 1 Apr to 31 Oct
daily 1–5pm. Jul & Aug 11am–
5pm except Sun. Adults £1.00,
Senior Citizens 60p, children 50p.

### Workhouse Museum
Sharow View, Allhallowgate,
Ripon, ☎ 01765 690799
Opening times: Under review.
Admission : Under review.

## SHOPS

### Antiques Centre
The Ginnel, Parliament Street,
☎ 01423 508857

### Couturiers of James Street and Parliament Street

### Farrah's Harrogate Toffee shop
31 Montpellier Parade
☎ 01423 525266

### McTague Fine Prints
17 Cheltenham Mount,
☎ 01423 567086

### Ogdens Jewellers
38 James Street, ☎ 01423 504123

### Richard Axe Books
12 Cheltenham Crescent,
☎ 01423 561867

### Woods Linens
Prince Albert Row, 65-67 Station
Parade, ☎ 01423 530111

### Petit Point (needlecraft)
12 Montpellier Parade,
☎ 01423 565632

## THEATRE

**Harrogate Theatre**, Oxford Street. ☎ 01423 502116
The building is closed on Sundays, and there are no performances on
Mondays. Concessions are available for children, the disabled, senior
citizens, students and the unwaged. Enquiries may be made at the box
office.

## TOURIST INFORMATION OFFICES

### Harrogate
Royal Baths Assembly Rooms,
Crescent Road,
Harrogate HG1 2RR.
☎ 01423 537300
Open all year.

### Boroughbridge
Fishergate. ☎ 01423 323373
Open Summer season.

### Knaresborough
9 Castle Courtyard, Market Place,
☎ 01423 866886
Open Summer season.

### Pateley Bridge
18 High Street, ☎ 01423 711147
Open Summer season.

### Ripon
Minster Road, ☎ 01765 604625
Open Summer season.

# INDEX

# LANDMARK
## Publishing Ltd ● ● ● ●

## VISITORS GUIDES

* Practical guides for the independent traveller
* Written in the form of touring itineraries
* Full colour illustrations and maps
* Detailed Landmark FactFile of practical information
* Landmark Visitors Guides highlight all the interesting places you will want to see, so ensuring that you make the most of your visit

1. *Britain*

| | |
|---|---|
| Cornwall | Jersey |
| Cotswolds & | Lake District |
| Shakespeare | Peak District |
| Country | Scotland |
| Devon | Somerset |
| Dorset | Southern Lakeland |
| East Anglia | Southern Peak District |
| Guernsey | Yorkshire Dales |
| Hampshire | York |

2. *Europe*

| | |
|---|---|
| Bruges | Provence |
| Cracow | Riga |
| Italian Lakes | Vilnius |
| Madeira | |

3. *Other*

Dominican Republic
Florida: Gulf Coast
Florida Keys
India: Goa
India: Kerala
  & The South
New Zealand
Orlando &
  Central Florida
St Lucia
The Gambia

### Landmark Publishing
Waterloo House, 12 Compton, Ashbourne, Derbyshire DE6 IDA England
Tel: 01335 347349  Fax: 01335 347303  e-mail: landmark@clara.net
Catalogue sent on request

Published by
**Landmark Publishing Ltd,**
Waterloo House, 12 Compton, Ashbourne, Derbyshire DE6 1DA England
Tel: 01335 347349  Fax: 01335 347303  e-mail: landmark@clara.net

1st Edition
ISBN 1 901 522 55 5

### Acknowledgements

Mr P Barnwell, for his advice on walks and rambles in the Harrogate District;
Mr M Hine, for his advice on Tourist Information in the Harrogate District,
and for supplying appropriate photographs;
Mr C McGonigle, for advice on parking and road traffic;
Mr G Robinson, Play Areas and Open Spaces Officer.

**Print:** UIC Printing & Packaging Pte Ltd, Singapore
**Cartography & Design:** Samantha Witham
**Editor:** Kay Coulson

**Front Cover:** Royal Baths, Harrogate
**Back cover, top:** Harrogate International Festival
**Back cover, bottom:** Fountains Abbey

**Picture Credits:**
**All photography supplied by Harrogate International Centre
except those mentioned below.**
Malcolm Neesam: 10 both, 12, 21 both, 22, 23, 44, 49
**Yorkshire Agricultural Society:** 15 both
**Harrogate International Festival:** Back cover top, 16, 17TL, 17TR
**Lindsey Porter:** 85